A B Brown
16 June 2004

THE ⲉPISTLES OF

FIRST, SECOND, & THIRD

JOHN & JUDE

FORGIVENESS,
LOVE, AND COURAGE

✹ AMG *Publishers*
CHATTANOOGA, TENNESSEE

TWENTY-FIRST CENTURY
BIBLICAL COMMENTARY SERIES

THE EPISTLES OF

FIRST, SECOND, & THIRD

JOHN & JUDE

FORGIVENESS,
LOVE, AND COURAGE

ROBERT
LIGHTNER

GENERAL EDITORS

MAL COUCH & ED HINDSON

ISBN 0-89957-813-6

Cover design by Phillip Rodgers, AMG Publishers
Interior design and typesetting by Warren Baker, AMG Publishers
Edited and Proofread by Warren Baker, Patrick Belvill, and Weller Editorial Services, Chippewa Lake, MI

Printed in the United States of America
08 07 06 05 04 03 –R– 7 6 5 4 3 2 1

To Philip and David, my grandsons,
with the prayer that both of you will hear
and obey what Jesus said to His Philip:
"Follow Me" (John 1:43)

Twenty-First Century Biblical Commentary Series

Mal Couch, Th.D., and Ed Hindson, D.Phil.

The New Testament has guided the Christian Church for over two thousand years. This one testament is made up of twenty-seven books, penned by godly men through the inspiration of the Holy Spirit. It tells us of the life of Jesus Christ, His atoning death for our sins, His miraculous resurrection, His ascension back to heaven, and the promise of His second coming. It also tells the story of the birth and growth of the Church and the people and principles that shaped it in its earliest days. The New Testament concludes with the book of Revelation pointing ahead to the glorious return of Jesus Christ.

Without the New Testament, the message of the Bible would be incomplete. The Old Testament emphasizes the promise of a coming Messiah. It constantly points us ahead to the One who is coming to be the King of Israel and the Savior of the world. But the Old Testament ends with this event still unfulfilled. All of its ceremonies, pictures, types, and prophecies are left awaiting the arrival of the "Lamb of God who takes away the sin of the world!" (John 1:29).

The message of the New Testament represents the timeless truth of God. As each generation seeks to apply that truth to its specific context, an up-to-date commentary needs to be created just for them. The editors and authors of the Twenty-First Century Biblical Commentary Series have endeavored to do just that. This team of scholars represents conservative, evangelical, and dispensational scholarship at its best. The individual authors may differ on minor points of interpretation, but all are convinced that the Old and New Testaments teach a dispensational framework for biblical history. They also hold to a pretribulational and premillennial understanding of biblical prophecy.

The French scholar René Pache reminded each succeeding generation, "If the power of the Holy Spirit is to be made manifest anew among us, it is of primary importance that His message should regain its due place. Then we shall be able to put the enemy to flight by the sword of the Spirit which is the Word of God."

Martin Luther said of John's epistles, "I have never read books more simple, yet sublime." They are letters written from a pastor's heart. John R. W. Stott observes: "John writes as a pastor to his people in a language every modern pastor will understand. He warns them, exhorts them, argues with them, and instructs them." As the sole survivor of the original disciples, John writes with a deliberate pastoral authority and demeanor. His letters are rooted and grounded in a practical local church ministry and serve as wonderful models of pastoral care for us today.

Jude's epistle is also one that springs from a heart of concern for the truth and its application to the lives of God's people. George Lawlor points out Jude's "dramatic and forceful manner of writing and his use of the Old Testament records to support his argument." Jude writes as a man of courage, conviction, and concern. In so doing, he calls upon believers in every generation to "contend earnestly for the faith."

Contents

SECTION 1

Forgiveness and Fellowship

The Book of First John

CHAPTER 1

Background of First John

Preview:
The truths in 1 John are primarily for children of God. It is a family epistle. Already in John's day many were denying and rejecting the faith once delivered to the saints. Christ is prominent in the book because He was the One being attacked by the false teachers. John also gives careful attention to the believer's responsibility to be in fellowship with God. The book has in it both positives and negatives with respect to the behavior of the child of God.
Unlike the apostle Paul, who wrote with lawyer-like logic, John's writing is more like the work of a musician. That is to say, he touches on a theme, leaves it to introduce other themes, and then returns repeatedly to those themes. Some of John's themes are primary and some secondary. For a full understanding of them, other Scripture passages must often be brought to bear on the subjects he introduces.

Authorship

Substantial evidence both internally and externally supports the apostle John as the human agent the Spirit of God used to pen this book. Internally, the language and style of 1 John are identical to that of the Gospel of John. Even though the gospel text does not name John the apostle as the author, there is little doubt that he was the author. Early church fathers as well as internal evidence clearly point to him.

The list is extremely long of all the church fathers who endorsed these epistles, quoted from them, and assigned John as the author. Quotes can be cited from Polycarp, Papias, Eusebius, Diognetus, Irenaeus, Clement of Alexandria, Tertullian, Origen, and even the Gnostic Carpocrates. The famous epistle entitled The Letter of the Churches of Vienne and Lyons, written in A.D. 177, includes allusions to this book. First John is also mentioned in other early documents, such as the Muratorian Canon, and is quoted in the Peshitta, or Syrian version of the New Testament.

Everett F. Harrison summarizes the evidence from the early church fathers:

> The earliest clear-cut case of dependence is in Polycarp's *Epistle to the Philippians* (chap. 7), where a virtual reproduction of 1 John 4:2 in concise form appears. There are probable allusions to the epistle in the *Didache*, in *Hermas* and in the *Epistle to Diognetus*. Irenaeus, in quoting 1 John 2:18–22, part of it accurately and the rest very freely, states that this is John's testimony in his epistle. Clement of Alexandria quotes from John's "greater epistle" several times in his *Stromateis* and in his *Quis Dives Salvetur*. In the Canon of Muratori, after a statement concerning the circumstances surrounding the origin of the Gospel according to John and some observations concerning differences in the Gospels, there is allusion to John's having written concerning the Lord in his epistles, followed by the quotation of a part of 1 John 1:1, concluding with a portion of verse 4. The testimony of the Fragment concerning other epistles by John is notoriously difficult to make out, but this must be reserved for later discussion. It is *not surprising* to find generous *use* of 1 John by Origen and Tertullian and the acknowledgment of its Johannine authorship. Finally, Eusebius indicates that the former (or first) of John's epistles had been accepted without dispute both by those of his (Eusebius') time and by the ancients. So 1 John had its place among the acknowledged writings, according to this Father of the church.[1]

Throughout all three of John's epistles we find signs that the author is the same person who wrote the Gospel of John, yet the author of all three documents is unwilling to speak of himself. Readers meet the writer as a calm narrator, an encourager of the sheep, an exhorter and teacher. With the same heightened calmness, diffidence, and composure, the Lord Jesus and Christian virtues are lifted up and presented to the recipients of the letters.

The author desires to counsel, warn, and remind readers to walk with a consciousness of their position in Christ. Confessing sin, walking in truth and love, avoiding a loose spiritual life, and being aware of the temptations of the world all stand as important themes of John. He speaks with intimate experience and manifest plainness because he had walked with Jesus.

Doubt of John's authorship is quickly dispelled when one looks at thirty-five passages from the fourth Gospel that show parallels and commonality in this first epistle. Wording, style, and expressions are alike in both works. Charles John Ellicott's commentary notes:

> The identity of ideas in both writings is of the same character; they bear no sign of imitation, but are the free production of the same spirit. Light, life, darkness, truth, the lie, propitiation, doing righteousness, doing sin, doing lawlessness, life and death, loving and hating, love of the Father and love of the world, children of God and children of the devil, the spirit of truth and the spirit of error: all these notions underlie the thought of both Gospel and Epistle.[2]

As well, the writer of both shows the same devotion and faithfulness to Christ. In both works stand dogmatic thoughts of one who was well aware of the commandments of Christ. The apostle does not mince words in his instructions to his readers. "It would, indeed, be difficult to find a more structural and penetrating identity between the works of any author whatever than there is between the Gospel and the First Epistle."[3]

Concerning this Johannine authorship, Henry Thiessen concludes:

> The author represents himself as an eye-witness of Christ (1:1–4; 4:14). . . . The ancient and unbroken testimony which ascribes the Epistle to the Apostle John also supports this view. The writer seems to stand in relationship to his readers as teacher and taught (cf. 1:2, 3). This theory accounts for the absence of the writer's name and other details about himself: they were superfluous, his thoughts, language, and emphasis were too well known to be mistaken.[4]

The term *Logos* applied to Christ in John's gospel, 1 John, and the book of Revelation argues for a Johannine authorship of all three. John the apostle is of course stated to be the author of the book of Revelation. The use of the reference to the Holy Spirit as the *Paraclete* in both the gospel and the epistle points also to John as the author of the first epistle. Finally, a rather large number of passages in the Gospel of John parallel those in the first epistle.

The author was the son of Zebedee and a fisherman (Mark 1:19–20; Luke 5:10). He was from the town or village of Salome (Matt. 27:56; Mark 15:40). John the apostle was the younger brother of James (Matt. 4:21). It is generally believed that John was brought to faith in Christ through the preaching of the faithful John the Baptist. John was especially close to Christ, being in what often has been called the "inner circle," made up of Peter, James, and John. He is referred to in the Gospel of John as the disciple whom Jesus loved.

Date of Writing

Nothing in the epistle indicates a specific date for its composition. Many conservatives suggest a date late in the first century. Other conservatives, however, argue for a much earlier date of between A.D. 60 and 65.[5]

The date of A.D. 90–95 seems more plausible. John spent the last years of his life in Ephesus, where he very likely wrote the epistle. The false teaching of Cerinthus, condemned in the epistle, was prominent in Asia Minor. There are no references in the epistle to seasons of persecution before or during the time it was written. If the destruction of Jerusalem in A.D. 70 had preceded the writing, it seems strange that no reference is made to it. Therefore, it is generally agreed that the writing was sometime after A.D. 70 but before the great persecution under Domitian and Trajan (A.D. 98–117).

Addressees

Again, this letter contains nothing about the ones for whom it was intended or even about their geographic location. It is clear, however, that the readers were Christians. If, as many believe, the book was written from Ephesus, we may assume it was intended for the local churches there. First John is usually viewed as a book circulated among the Christians in Ephesus.

The readers could be Gentiles, on the basis of the final admonition to keep themselves from idols (5:21). But it is possible that the word "idols" is not being used in a concrete sense of actual idolatry. The author may have in mind the chimeras of false teaching, which are as empty and misleading as the objects before which the pagans bow. J. A. T. Robinson points out that in contrast to the Pauline epistles, where so much is made of the need of confessing Jesus as Lord, 1 John is silent on this score, but gives prominence to the confession of Jesus as the Christ (2:22). This favors the same general milieu for the epistles of John as for the Gospel, namely, Greek-speaking Jews. Only in this case the recipients are clearly adherents of the faith and need only to be assured and confirmed in it.[6]

Theme

John's theme for the "little children" (2:1) is each believer's fellowship with God and other believers. A three-dimensional fellowship is apparent in the book. Each believer is exhorted to be in fellowship with God and also with other believers.

Another ongoing theme in 1 John is *belief*. This was also a distinct subject in the Gospel of John where the verb *to believe* is used some ninety-five times but the noun *belief* is not even used once. The word is used eleven times as a verb in 1 John and only twice as a noun, translated *faith*. However, when John thinks of believers being *committed* to Christ, he uses the adjective *faithful* eleven times throughout his writings, except in 2 John (John 20:27; 1 John 1:9; 3 John 5; Rev. 1:5; 2:10, 13; 3:14; 17:14; 19:11; 21:5; 22:6).

John sees faith as an active virtue, beginning with salvation trust, and then expressed in and lived out through the Christian walk. Zuck writes:

> The first mention of belief in 1 John actually occurs in 1:6–7, "If we claim to have fellowship with him yet walk in the darkness, we lie and do not live by the truth. But if we walk in the light, as he is in the light, we have fellowship with one another, and the blood of Jesus, his Son, purifies us from all sin." In these two verses John employed no less than three sets of images referring to genuine belief: "Walking in darkness" as the antithesis of walking in the light denotes the person who has not come to the light, that is, one who has not come to Jesus, the Light of the world (cf. John 3:19–21). This person, for John, is an unbeliever regardless of whatever claims one may make about having fellowship with God.[7]

A *negative* way of speaking about belief is found in 1 John 4:1 where the apostle writes, "Do not believe every spirit, but test the spirits to see whether they are from God." The negative spirits would be those coming from the propagation of lies, from demons, or from Satan. John also warns of the *principle* of antichrist, that is, the philosophy that denies the very deity and person of the Lord Jesus. The *positive* spirits would probably refer to the attitudes and holiness of the writings of the ancient prophets, also whether what they wrote conformed to truth found throughout the Old Testament—in other words, whether their messages are fully confirmed and have stood the test of time but, as well, whether they reflect the full scope of predictive revelation.

> The pressing issue before John's readers was how they could recognize such messages as originating from God or from the spirit of the antichrist (cf. v. 6). "Being born of God" and "knowing God" (v. 7) are further descriptions of genuine belief that have occurred before in the epistle (2:3–4; 3:9). In this context John spoke of "believing" the love that God has for the readers as believers (4:16, "rely on").[8]

First John and the Gospel of John

First John and the Gospel of John bear both similarities and differences. A major difference is that John's Gospel assumes our Lord's humanity while it stresses His deity. The epistle, on the other hand, stresses Jesus' humanity while it assumes His deity.

Harrison provides a summary of similarities:

That a great similarity exists between the two writings is apparent to every reader. It shows itself (a) in the vocabulary. Important words common to both are: Father, Son, Spirit, beginning, Word (Logos), Paraclete, believe, life, eternal, love, remain (abide), keep, commandment, true (*alēthinos*), know *(ginōskō* and *oida)*, have, beget, witness, light, darkness, world, sin, devil.

It appears (b) in larger units, such as the only begotten Son (4:9; cf. 3:16, 18), the Savior of the world (4:14; cf. 4:42), the Spirit of truth (4:6; cf. 14:17; 15:26; 16:13), doing the truth (1:6; cf. 3:21), to be "of the truth" (3:19; cf. 18:37), to be "of God" (3:10; cf. 8:47), to be "born of God" (3:9; cf. 1:13), the children of God (3:2; cf. 11:52), to "walk in darkness" (2:11; cf. 8:12), children of the devil (3:10; cf. 8:44), no man has ever seen God (4:12; cf. 1:18), to give his life (3:16; cf. 10:11), to pass from death to life (3:14; cf. 5:24), to overcome the world (5:4; cf. 16:33), water and blood (5:6; cf. 19:34), to do sin (3:4; cf. 8:34), to take away sin (3:5; cf. 1:29), to know and believe (4:16; cf. 6:69), to remain for ever (2:17; cf. 8:35).[9]

The Gnostic Issues

Harrison summarizes well the Gnostic issues in the book:

A prominent feature of Gnosticism was its claim to special illumination and higher knowledge by which one rose into true fellowship with God by mystical contemplation. This could work to the depreciation of faith as elementary and inadequate, and may account for the frequent insistence in 1 John that Christians, supposedly limited by mere faith, actually have all the knowledge of God and of spiritual things that is available to men (2:20–21).

If the doctrine of the Gnostics needed refutation, so did their practice. If God is light (this the Gnostics proclaimed), then one must walk in the light if he would have fellowship with him. It will not do to profess a sinlessness based on the rapport of the spirit with God to the neglect of what is actually done in the body (1:8,10). To talk about love for God based on a lofty mystical speculation and at the same time to fall miserably in love for the brethren (4:20; cf. 3:7–8) is contrary to reason and revelation alike.[10]

For more on Gnosticism, see appendix 3.

Purposes of the Book

John stated several of his purposes in writing to the "little children" (1 John 2:12), or more literally, the "little born ones."

Harrison gives the overall purpose of the epistle:

> Perhaps the best starting point is the statement of the writer that certain people who had formerly been associated with the Christian community or communities being addressed have now gone out from the believers and by that withdrawal have made it clear that they were not really a part of the Christian church (2:19). In fact, the previous verse speaks of many antichrists, as though to label these false teachers. They are still a problem, for their teaching has evidently been widely sown and needs to be repudiated and exposed. An ingredient of this false teaching is the denial that Jesus is the Christ (2:22; cf. 5:1). Another, apparently, is the denial that Jesus Christ has come in the flesh (4:2–3). This also bears the antichrist label (4:3). Taken together, these passages hint that the source of trouble, if unitary in character, was Gnostic with a Jewish flavor. Men of this stripe would be concerned with the issue of Jesus' Messiahship and would also be expected to deny the incarnation. Gnosticism, with its insistence on the evil character of matter, could not tolerate the teaching that the Son of God had come in flesh to dwell among men. That a combination of Judaic and Gnostic elements could be made is apparent from the Colossian epistle.[11]

However, there are other more specific purposes for writing this letter.

To Provide Fellowship and Joy (1:3–4). The key thought of the very first verse of the epistle is enlarged in verses 3 and 4. John wanted his readers to have fellowship with him and his partners (v. 3). John and the believers to whom he wrote had many things in common. However, the very most important thing was their fellowship with God the Father and with His Son Jesus Christ.

When the readers would understand the wonderful relationship they had with the Father and the Son and their fellowship with others of like precious faith, their joy would be made full (v. 4).

The word *fellowship (koinōnia)* is used by John mainly in 1 John, in a positive sense (1:3, 6, 7). Using *koinōnia* only once in a negative way, he warns believers not to have fellowship (be participating) in the evil deeds of deceivers (2 John 11). Only in 1 John 1:3 does he use the word to describe fellowship among believers, but then also with God the Father and with Jesus. The apostle says he desires "that you [believers] also may have fellowship with us; and indeed our fellowship is with the Father, and with His Son Jesus Christ."

Paul's Use of the Greek Word Koinonia

The Greek Christians made **a contribution** for the poor (Rom. 15:26; 2 Cor. 9:13).

The child of God is called into **fellowship** with God's Son, Jesus Christ (1 Cor. 1:9).

The Lord's Supper symbolizes **a sharing** in the blood of Christ (1 Cor. 10:16).

What partnership, or what **fellowship**, has light with darkness? (2 Cor. 6:14).

The **fellowship** of the Holy Spirit be with you all (2 Cor. 13:14; Phil. 2:1).

The right hand of **fellowship** (Gal. 2:9).

Your **participation** in the gospel (Phil. 1:5).

To know Jesus and the **fellowship** of His sufferings (Phil. 3:10).

To Prevent Sin (2:1). John becomes very personal in chapter 2. He did not want his little children to sin. In the first chapter the readers were informed about how to be restored to fellowship with God when they sinned (1:9). John did not want to be misunderstood. The reason for his writing to them was not to discourage them or to make them content in their sin. Rather, he wrote so they would learn not to commit sin.

To Promote Love (2:5-10). One of the central themes of 1 John is love—God's love for His own and the believers' love for one another. God's command for His people to love one another is both old and new (vv. 7-8). John wrote to his believing readers to promote love.

To Proclaim Forgiveness (2:12). The readers must have needed a reminder of what God had done for them when He saved them by His grace. He forgave them of all their sins. God did this "for His name's sake." They, like all believers, needed to hear the message of God's forgiveness over and over again. John wrote to announce the message of forgiveness loud and clear.

To Prepare Believers for Opposition (2:26). John believed that to be forewarned was to be forearmed. The little children needed to keep in mind that Satan was their fiercest foe. He was and still is the great seducer. It appears that satanic seduction had already begun among the readers. To stop the deception, John wrote about how God's people could be prepared to face Satan's onslaught of evil.

To Provide a Basis for Assurance (5:13). The Spirit of God led John to write his first epistle to instruct the people about the assurance of salvation God wanted them to have. This was especially needed in view of the presence of antichrists and other false teachers promoting their false doctrines among them. The readers were secure in Christ, and they needed to be assured of it. Albert Barnes sees several main characteristics about the book:

(1) It is full of love. The writer dwells on it; places it in a variety of attitudes; enforces the duty of loving one another by a great variety of considerations, and shows that it is essential to the vary nature of religion. (2) The epistle abounds with statements on the evidences of piety, or the characteristics of true [belief]. The author seems to have felt that those to whom he wrote were in danger of embracing false notions . . . of being seduced by the abettors of error.[12]

Outline of First John

I. Fellowship with God (1 John 1:1-7)

A. Declaration of Fellowship with God (1:1-4)

1. Christ's humanity (1:1)

2. Christ's deity (1:2)

3. Reasons for the declaration (1:3-4)

B. Description of Fellowship with God (1:5-6)

C. Delight of Fellowship with God (1:7)

II. Sin and the Child of God (1 John 1:8—2:6)

A. The Reality of the Believer's Sin (1:8, 10)

B. The Remedy for the Believer's Sin (1:9; 2:1-2)

C. The Reminder to the Believers (2:3-6)

III. Fellowship with God and the Believer's Walk (1 John 2:7-17)

A. The Commandment (2:7-8)

B. The Positive Aspect of the Commandment (2:9-11)

C. The Purpose of the Commandment (2:12-14)

D. The Negative Aspect of the Commandment (2:15-17)

IV. Antichrists in the Last Hour (1 John 2:18-27)

A. The Reality of Antichrists (2:18-19)

B. The Recognition of Antichrists (2:20-23)

C. The Refuge from the Antichrists' Teaching (2:24-27)

V. Fellowship with the Lord and His Return (1 John 2:28—3:3)

CHAPTER 2

Fellowship with God
1 John 1:1-7

Preview:

The word koinōnia, fellowship, means more than friendly social relations. Partnership is the primary idea conveyed by the word. It refers to two parties who possess and partake of something in common. Companionship would be a secondary meaning. John claims for God's people partnership with God the Father and with God the Son. He speaks also of the need for fellowship or partnership of believers with other believers.

The apostle Peter described regeneration using the word koinōnia, and it is translated "partaker" (2 Pet. 1:4). Peter also used the term in 1 Peter 4:13 of sharing in the sufferings of Christ. Paul used the same word to convey the same idea (cf. Phil. 3:10 and 2 Tim. 1:8). These usages by Peter and Paul verify the meaning of partnership as used by John in his first epistle.

Declaration of Fellowship with God (1:1–4)

What is the basis on which the child of God can have fellowship with the God of the entire universe? In the opening verses of John's first epistle, he answers this question. The basis for the believer's fellowship with God is in the person of God's own dear Son, the Lord Jesus Christ.

The genuine humanity of Christ was not only questioned but also denied by some whose false teaching was being heard by the little children to whom John wrote. The apostle therefore began his epistle by defending the true humanity of Christ.

Christ's Humanity (1:1)

Three great beginnings are referred to in Scripture. In Genesis 1:1 "the beginning" refers to the beginning of time. "In the beginning" in John 1:1 speaks of eternity before the universe was. In 1 John 1:1 "the beginning" refers to the beginning of the Christian era and relates the Savior to His life on earth. In other words, John wrote in his gospel of the preincarnate Christ and in His first epistle of the incarnate Christ.

> This is such language as John would use respecting him, and indeed the phrase "the beginning," as applicable to the Lord Jesus, is peculiar to John in the writings of the New Testament; and the language here may be regarded as one proof that this epistle was written by him, for it is just such an expression as he would use.[1]

John began with a relative pronoun in the neuter gender, "what" (1 John 1:1). The things named cannot be separated from Christ personally. Each one of the things concerns Christ's genuine humanity—"we have heard . . . we have seen . . . and our hands handled."

> That is pertaining to his person, and to what he did. "I have seen *him*; seen what he was as a man; how he appeared on earth; and I have seen whatever there was in his works to indicate his character and origin." John professes there to have seen enough in this respect to furnish evidence that he was the Son of God. It is not hearsay on which he relies, but he had the testimony of his own eyes in [this] case.[2]

The incipient seeds of Gnosticism were already starting to sprout among John's readership. This later developed into a very serious false teaching. Those who held Gnostic ideas were called Gnostics, and their name was derived from the Greek word meaning "to know" or "knowledge." These people claimed to have superior knowledge and believed they alone possessed true knowledge, which they also believed was salvific. The Gnostics also denied Christ's real humanity. To them Christ appeared to be human but really was not. Foundational to the Gnostic beliefs was their dualistic philosophy—matter was evil and spirit was good.

John set forth three strong evidences for the true and genuine humanity of Christ. First, he and the other disciples "heard" Christ speak (1:1). By using the perfect tense with this word, John stressed that he and others had heard Christ speak repeatedly. Second, the sense of sight was another evidence for Christ's humanity. "Seen" (v. 1) denotes perception and vision. It appears that John had a particular instance in mind of when he had seen Jesus. Third, John adds to the hearing and seeing of Christ the fact that he and the other disciples actually "handled" Christ—that is, touched Him with their hands (v. 1). Very likely, John had in mind the appearances of Christ after His resurrection that demonstrated to John and the other disciples that the body placed in the grave was the same body brought forth from the grave (cf. Luke 24:39).

The designation Word *(Logos)* attracts our attention. What does it mean? What picture does it convey of the Lord Jesus? Let me illustrate: I might have all kinds of ideas, thoughts, suggestions in my mind, all kinds of emotions in my heart, but unless there was some way, some means by which I could convey them to others, they would not know them. This is where words derive their value. Words are vehicles for conveying thoughts to others, and if it is true that "as a man thinketh in his heart so is he" then my words will be vehicles for conveying to others what I am. The Lord Jesus is the Word, the conveyor to men not only of the thoughts of God and the wisdom of God, but the conveyor of what God is. He is the vehicle to reveal God to men, thus "no man hath seen God at any time; the only begotten Son, which is in the bosom of the Father (who has His being in the bosom of the Father), he hath declared him" (John 1:18). As the "Word" our Lord Jesus revealed God in His power in the creation (John 1:3) and upholding of the world (Heb. 1:1-3). He has revealed Him through incarnation (John 1:14) and redemption to the guilty sons of men. Did He not say: "He that hath seen me hath seen the Father" (John 14:9)?[3]

704 8660 8873
Michelle Summitt

Christ's Deity (1:2)

Only God possesses eternal life. Since John speaks of Christ as "the eternal life, which was with the Father," this verse therefore assigns full and absolute deity to Christ. This is the One said to be heard, seen, and touched. He was and is the God-man.

The preposition translated "with" is very significant as used here (1:2). It implies fellowship. Kenneth Wuest summarized its use in these words: It "means that the life here referred to is a Person, for it requires a person to have fellowship. . . . The life here is none other than the Lord Jesus Himself who is said by John to have been in fellowship with the Father."[4]

Reasons for the Declaration (1:3-4)

In these verses John revisits the theme he introduced in 1:1. Here in verses 3 and 4 he tells his readers one of the purposes for writing to them about the things he and others heard and saw concerning Christ. The apostle wrote so that his readers could enjoy fellowship with him and his coworkers—apostolic witnesses. Albert Barnes well states:

> We announce it, or make it known unto you—referring either to what he purposes to say in this epistle, or more probably embracing all that he had written respecting him, and supposing that his Gospel was in their hands. He means to call their attention on the subject, in order to counteract the errors which began to prevail.[5]

"Fellowship" (v. 3) is the translation of *koinōnia* that conveys the idea of sharing. In the context here it refers to a very special kind of sharing—entering into what John and the other apostles experienced with Christ. In addition to that firsthand experience, John adds, "Our fellowship is with the Father" (v. 3). "This is a stunning claim. The author of the epistle is stating that he is a part of a circle so intimate with God that if one has fellowship with his circle, one has fellowship with God the Father and with His Son."[6]

A second purpose for John's letter follows in verse 4: "So that our joy may be made complete." Apparently the joy of John's readers was not complete. No doubt, the confusing false teaching that was circulating concerning Christ discouraged them. Christ had taught John and the other apostles the importance of abiding in Him so that His joy might remain in them (John 15:11 cf. 16:24).

Description of Fellowship with God (1:5–6)

John has stated clearly how Christ, the eternal life, was presented or manifested (1:1–4). Now he sets forth the message Christ proclaimed: "And this is the message we have heard from Him and announce to you, that God is light, and in Him there is no darkness at all" (v. 5). Light and darkness "are used metaphorically in Scripture in several senses. Intellectually, light is truth and darkness is ignorance or error. Morally, light is purity and darkness evil (i.e., Prov. 6:23; Ps. 119:105; 2 Pet. 1:19)."[7] This clear statement about God's character describes His absolutely holy nature, totally free of moral defects.

God Himself is the standard by which believers must conduct themselves as they seek to live out the Christian life—to be in fellowship with God. Some in John's day were promoting the idea that Christians could disregard God's laws. The result of such teaching and living, of course, leads to lawlessness and license to sin. It is also a terrible distortion of the biblical teaching of the believer's liberty in Christ. This false teaching formed the background of John's declarations about God.

If God condoned or approved sin, even in the life of a believer, it would imply that there is evil in Him. He certainly would then be less than holy.

"God is light" (1:5), John declared. There is no definite article with the word *light*, which means God in His very nature and essence is light. Throughout Scripture light refers to holiness and is in direct contrast to sin or darkness. Christ's declaration then that God is light speaks of the Father's absolute holiness. Therefore, to think such a God would allow sin or lawlessness to go unjudged is unthinkable. With double emphasis John added the phrase, "In Him there is no darkness at all" (v. 5). More literally, this statement would read, "In Him is no darkness at all, not even the smallest portion of it." God Himself, therefore, is the standard for holy living.

The barrier to holy living is sin. Believers cannot sin and have fellowship with God at the same time, yet it appears that some of John's readers were thinking this was possible. John countered such false teaching in no uncertain terms: "If we say we have fellowship with Him and yet walk in darkness, we lie and do not practice the truth" (1:6). The two—fellowship with God and walking in darkness—are mutually exclusive. Believers who claim to be in partnership with God yet continue to walk or live in darkness are simply belying their claims.

The verb translated "walk" (v. 6) is in the present tense and the subjunctive mood in Greek. The reference therefore seems to be to continuous, habitual sinning. Sin is the habit of the person's life John is referring to in his hypothetical case. The entire lifestyle and behavior of this person is lived in the realm of darkness.[8]

FELLOWSHIP: The New Testament Teaching
- *The early church began with the apostles' teaching and fellowship (Acts 2:42).*
- *Believers are called to have fellowship with God's Son (1 Cor. 1:9).*
- *Believers are not to have fellowship with darkness (2 Cor. 6:14).*
- *Believers are to have fellowship with the Holy Spirit (2 Cor. 13:14; Phil. 2:1).*
- *Believers are to experience the fellowship or sharing in Christ's suffering (Phil. 3:10).*
- *Believers are to have a fellowship of faith (Philem. 1:6).*

Delight of Fellowship with God (1:7)

In 1:6 John set forth a hypothetical case, but in verse 7 he turned to an actual one. "But if we walk in the light as He Himself is in the light, we have fellowship with one another, and the blood of Jesus His Son cleanses us from all sin." John takes his readers beyond the affirmation that "God is light" (v. 5) to "He Himself is in the light" (v. 7). "To walk in the light must mean essentially to live in God's presence, exposed to what He has revealed about Himself. This, of course, is done through openness in prayer and through openness to the Word of God in which He is revealed."[9]

The "one another" (1:7) refers to the believer and God. When we walk or live in the light, in other words, we have fellowship with God and He is with us. What a thrill it is to have something in common with God—light, or holiness. How can this be? It can only be true because as we walk in the light we not only have fellowship with God, but the blood of His Son keeps on cleansing us from all sin. The cleansing referred to here is the ongoing cleansing and forgiveness Christians need to experience (v. 9), not the forgiveness experienced at the time of salvation (Eph. 1:7).

Study Questions

1. How is 1 John 1:1 compared to Genesis 1:1?

2. How is 1 John 1:1 compared to John 1:1?

3. Who were the Gnostics, and what were some of their beliefs?

4. Can sin and fellowship be compatible within the believer at the same time?

5. In what way is the blood of Christ "keeping on" in its cleansing work of the believer?

CHAPTER 3

Sin and the Child of God
1 John 1:8–2:6

Preview:

The Scriptures clearly teach that believers sin. Some theologians, however, teach that at the time of God's second work of grace in a saved person's life, the sin nature is eradicated. After this experience, which is sometimes referred to as the baptism of the Holy Spirit, the believer no longer commits sins of commission but is not entirely free of sins of omission. Such teaching is not in harmony with the teaching of Scripture.

Sin may be defined as anything that does not conform to God's character. The usual lists of sins that Christians compile are incomplete. As we have already seen from 1 John, God is and must be the standard by which we measure or judge our conduct. God's person is revealed in His Word and is the criterion of judgment as to what is and is not sin. Not every specific sin is described in the Bible, and it is not necessary that every one be described, because God is revealed there, and He is the One with whom our behavior is to be compared. "You shall be holy, for I the LORD your God am holy" (Lev. 19:2; cf. 1 Pet. 1:16). The Greek word for sin, hamartia, means to miss the mark. That is what sin is, but it is more than that: It is also hitting the wrong mark. Sin is not just failing to do the right thing; it is also succeeding in doing the wrong thing.

The Reality of the Believer's Sin (1:8, 10)

The first thing John does as he approaches the subject of sin with his believing readers is stress that believers do sin. They do so because they still possess the capacity and tendency to sin, which theologians call the sin nature. The singular "sin" as opposed to "sins" (1:9) supports the sin principle in verse 8.

Those in John's day, and in every day since, who deny that they sin deceive no one but themselves. In addition to such self-deception, they do not speak the truth. "If we say that we have no sin, we are deceiving ourselves, and the truth is not in us" (v. 8). This last phrase, "the truth is not in us," has the same meaning as "we lie" (v. 6).

Again, John presents a hypothetical situation just as he did in verse 6. And again, as in verse 6, he is talking about believers. We know this because he uses the first person pronouns *we* and *us*. Those outside of Christ are not in view here. The believers John addressed were being influenced by those Zane C. Hodges calls "the Revisionists" or "Proto-Gnostics."[1] He hesitates to call them Gnostics because there does not seem to be any trace of Gnostic mythologies in 1 John. Some, however, do see such Gnostic teaching being opposed in the book.[2]

The Gnostics (from the Greek word meaning "to know" or "knowledge") believed matter was evil and spirit was good. They thus embraced a dualistic philosophy of life. In addition they also claimed superior knowledge, which they believed was the way of salvation. Because they believed matter—and thus the human body—was evil, they refused to believe Christ possessed a genuine human body. Christ, they said, *appeared* to be human; that is, He seemed to be human but was not.

Since these full-blown beliefs of the Gnostics were not yet developed at the time of the writing of John's epistles, it seems best to say that the incipient seeds of Gnosticism were sown earlier and were just beginning to sprout when John wrote. The effects of the early stages of the apostasy of the *revisionists* were already causing havoc among the recipients of John's epistles.

First John 1:9, which we will discuss after verse 10, deals with what we will call the remedy for the believer's sin. This verse presents a third hypothetical case, "If we say." The first case in verse 6 dealt with the impossibility of being a joint partner with God and continuing in sin at the same time. The second, in verse 8, sets forth the lie of those who deny the indwelling sin principle or nature. The third "If we say" deals with the believer's denial of individual acts of sin.

Such a denial makes God a liar and demonstrates that His Word is not in the one who engages in such denial. Simply put, this means that if the believer refuses to confess the sin the light of God (v. 7) reveals to him or her, such a response makes God a liar. Why? Because the testimony of His Word has been denied, which amounts to saying God has not been truthful with us.

"His word is not in us" (v. 10) does not speak of an unsaved state. Rather, in this context it means that God's Word is not effecting a change when it is not believed. In other words, it does not have control in us because its message has been rejected.

The Remedy for the Believer's Sin (1:9; 2:1-2)

That God has made provision for the forgiveness of the believer's sin is further evidence of the reality of that sin. The believer's responsibility with regard to his or her sins committed as a child of God is clearly stated in 1:9: "If we confess our sins, He is faithful and righteous to forgive us our sins and to cleanse us from all unrighteousness." Since John makes it clear by the description of his readers as "children," "little children," and "beloved," application of verse 9 to nonbelievers as a means of salvation is totally without basis in fact.

Just as people are responsible to trust in the Lord Jesus Christ alone for salvation, so are they charged with the responsibility to agree with God concerning daily sin. When this is done, the Father's provision for daily cleansing through the gift of His Son is appropriated and is effective.

"Confess" is from the Greek *homologeō*, which means to agree with another, to say the same thing about something. Feeling guilty is not confession; nor is feeling sorry for sin. These emotions may accompany confession, but they do not define it. Children of God are called upon to agree with God's viewpoint of their sin. This means that however big or small the sin may be, it is to be viewed as a horrible offense against the very character of God. *Confess* is in the present tense, suggesting that this agreement with God about sin is to be the believer's constant heart attitude toward it.

The exhortation to confess our sins is accompanied with a twofold promise: "He is faithful and righteous to forgive us our sin and to cleanse us from all unrighteousness." "To forgive" (Greek, *aphiēmi*), means to send away, or dismiss, to no longer hold something against someone. At the time of salvation, the believing sinner is forgiven (Eph. 1:7). Positionally and permanently the child of God is forgiven because of Christ's substitution for him or her. Although all believers, while here on earth, have the forgiven position and are seated in the heavenlies in Christ, they still need daily forgiveness of sins. Kenneth Wuest contrasts the two aspects of forgiveness thusly: "Therefore, sin in a Christian's life is a matter, not between a lawbreaker and a judge, but between a child and his father."[3]

Because God is faithful and righteous, He not only responds to confession with forgiveness, He also cleanses the repentant believer from all unrighteousness (1:9). The aorist tense used with this verb indicates an immediate and single act of cleansing. There is also the clear implication in the phrase "cleanse us from all unrighteousness" the idea of God's dealing even with those sins of which we are not aware. The reference to "all unrighteousness" implies this wonderful truth.[4]

The believer's responsibility stated so clearly in 1:9 is based solidly on the divine provision stated in 2:1–2. That provision—a person, God's Son, Jesus Christ the righteous (2:1)— is the same for believers and unbelievers. No other fount of cleansing has been opened for sin and uncleanness.

The little children addressed must not think that since sin was certain among them, it should be of no great concern to them. John wrote so they, and we by application, may not sin (2:1). *Advocate* is from the Greek *parakletos*, used of the Holy Spirit in John 14:16. It refers to someone called to the side of someone else to give aid. Jesus Christ is the believer's advocate before the Father. It seems clear that individual acts of sin, rather than a life of stubborn habitual sin, are in view in 2:1.

Christ is the altogether righteous One who can and does plead for the acquittal of the believer who sins. Our Lord's work as the believer's advocate relates to His work of intercession (Heb. 7:25). His work of intercession is designed to keep the believer from sinning. His work as advocate becomes effective when the believer sins in rebellion against God's desire that he not sin. Christ then, in this passage, is the believer's divine defense attorney.

The remedy for the believer's sins rests solidly on the faithfulness and righteousness of Christ (1:9) and His ministry as the believer's advocate (2:1). In addition Christ is the believer's propitiation for his or her sins (2:2). Propitiation, from the Greek *hilasmos*, means satisfaction. Christ Himself is the child of God's satisfaction based on His sacrificial death for sin.

John enlarges the recipients of Christ's work of propitiation to include "the whole world" (2:2). John the Baptist introduced Israel's Messiah at the very beginning of His public ministry as "the Lamb of God who takes away the sin of the world" (John 1:29). Greek scholar Zane Hodges describes the "tortured efforts" to make "the whole world" here as the world of the elect futile.[5] Christ paid the price, making provision for the salvation of every member of Adam's lost race.

> The phrase, "the whole world," is one which naturally embraces all men; is such as would be used if it be supposed that the apostle *meant* to teach that Christ died for all men; and is such as cannot be explained on any other supposition. If he died only for the elect, it is not true that he is the "propitiation for the sins of the whole world" in any proper sense, nor would it be possible then to assign a sense in which it could be true.[6]

Mal Couch writes:

> A Limited Atonement advocate would argue that John is saying that Christ was the propitiation for us as a group of the elect. But, oh yes, He is also the propitiation for the rest of the "elect," the world, who are scattered

around the globe! With a normal and a common sense method of observation, with no axes to grind, this verse could not be interpreted in that way. The first reading is a good reading! John makes it obvious that Christ's sacrifice is efficacious for those who are chosen, called, enlightened, and now believe, but it is also sufficient to save the whole world (Greek, *holou tou kosmou*).[7]

New Testament Commandments

- Christ commanded believers to love one another (John 15:17).
- Peter was instructed to pass on the commandments of Christ (Acts 10:33).
- Christ commanded Paul and Barnabas to be lights to the Gentiles (Acts 13:47).
- The commandment of Christ to love is both an old and a new commandment (1 John 2:7–11; 3:23; 4:21; 2 John 5).
- To please the Lord we keep His commandments (1 John 3:22, 24).
- To please the Lord we are to believe in Him (1 John 3:23).
- The Lord's commandments are not burdensome (1 John 5:3).
- Believers are commanded to walk in truth (2 John 1:4).
- Believers are commanded to walk in love (2 John 1:6).

The Reminder to the Believers (2:3–6)

Evangelical commentators differ over how we are to understand the words *know* and *commandments* in 2:3. "By this we know that we have come to know Him, if we keep His commandments." Is the reference to saving knowledge or experiential knowledge? Are the commandments the Old Testament laws, especially the Ten Commandments, or are they commands or charges given by Christ?

Those who understand "knowing" in reference to salvation insist that assurance of salvation comes by obeying either the Old Testament laws or the commands of Christ in the New Testament. Those of the Reformed covenant persuasion generally see commandments as referring to the Ten Commandments, which they believe are still binding on believers as a rule of life. Interestingly, the word translated commandments is not the Greek *nomos,* which John reserves for the Mosaic Law. It is rather *entolē,* meaning order, command, or change. Dispensationalists, on the other hand, do not believe the Law of Moses is binding upon believers today as a rule of life, as the way by which God deals with His people (2 Cor. 3:7–11; Heb. 7:11–14).[8] They therefore see the "commandments" (1 John 2:3) as the teachings of Christ recorded in the New Testament.

Contextually, it seems clear that John is still dealing with the believer's fellowship with God—the very theme of the entire epistle. He is seeking to answer the question he anticipates from his readers. What is that question? It is, "How may I be certain and how may I know in experience that Christ is my advocate and my propitiation?" The questions he is seeking to answer seem clear enough in the context.

This writer believes the primary meaning of the verses before us must be ascertained in harmony with the context. This means that John is not talking in 2:3 about saving knowledge. Rather, he is referring to knowledge gained by walking in the light. It is an intimate knowledge of who God the Father and God the Son really are. Christ the Son does seem to be the antecedent of the personal pronoun *Him* in 2:3. After all, He is the One who is the propitiation for the believer's sins in verse 2.

Those who make it the habit of their lives to walk in disobedience have reason to question whether or not they are in the faith. Divine life will manifest itself some way some time in one who possesses it. So obedience to the Word is a reason to have assurance of salvation. The most important basis for assurance, however, comes from the statements of Scripture to all who have trusted Christ alone for salvation. The songwriter Edward Mote had it right when he wrote, "My hope is built on nothing less than Jesus' blood and righteousness; I dare not trust the sweetest frame, but wholly lean on Jesus' name."

John did not call upon his readers to examine and judge one another as to the matter of obedience. Each one needs to examine his or her own life and personally answer the question, "Am I keeping God's commandments?" Obedience to our Lord's commandments is a test of whether we are walking in the Light (cf. 1:6, 8, 10).

"Keep" (2:3) is from the Greek *tēreō* and means to guard carefully, to observe, to be concerned that we do not disobey anything commanded of us by God. Wuest says the word speaks "of a solicitous desire that we do not disobey any of them [commandments] but on the other hand, that we obey them perfectly."[9]

Number of Times John Uses the Word "Love" in His Writings

- *The Gospel of John (56)*
- *1 John (46)*
- *2 John (4)*
- *3 John (3)*

"The one who says" (v. 4) makes clear that some must have been falsely claiming to know Christ experientially without observable obedience that should accompany such a claim. John uses "If we say" and "If someone says" a number of times in this book, indicating that such false claims were common.

Those who keep God's Word have the love of God perfected in them (v. 5). It appears certain that John is referring in verse 4 to those who had been given instruction and training in God's Word. He describes these as those who claim to "have come to know Him." Instruction in Scripture takes time.

The contrast in verse 5 is between "whoever keeps His word" and those who claim to know but do not keep God's Word. God's love is perfected in one who keeps His word. That is, the intent of God's love has been realized; it has been brought to its intended goal. When we have experienced God's love, we have confirmation that we are in Him.

John the Apostle: The Teaching of Love

God loves the world (John 3:16).

Have God's love in yourselves (John 5:42).

Jesus loves His disciples (John 13:23).

To love Christ is to keep His words (John 13:24).

Love one another (John 13:34).

The one who loves Jesus is loved by the Father (John 14:21).

Believers are to abide in Christ's love (John 15:9).

Believers are to abide in the Father's love (John 15:10).

The Father loves the Son (John 17:26).

To love the world is not to love God (1 John 2:15).

We know Christ loves us because He died for us (1 John 3:16).

Everyone who loves God is born of God (1 John 4:7).

God loves us and sent His Son to be a propitiation for us (1 John 4:10).

Christ abides with us if we love one another (1 John 4:12).

God is love (1 John 4:16).

Love is to be perfected (matured) in us (1 John 4:17).

We love because He first loved us (1 John 4:19).

We should love God's children (1 John 5:2).

The believer's walk is implied in the word *abides* (2:6). This word means more than a stated position. It carries the idea of remaining in communion and fellowship with Christ (see John 15). Again, John calls for the believer's practice to be in harmony with his or her claims. "Ought" comes from a Greek word that involves obligation or debt.

Study Questions

1. What does Zane C. Hodges mean when he writes of the Revisionists and Proto-Gnostics?

2. What kind of *confession* is John writing about in 1 John 1:9; 2:1–2?

3. What does confession do for the child of God? Why is confession important?

4. What does it mean for a believer to stumble?

5. What does it mean that Christ is our advocate, and what role is He fulfilling?

6. What does it mean for the love of God to be truly "perfected" in the believer who keeps His Word?

CHAPTER 4

Fellowship with God and the Believer's Walk
1 John 2:7-17

Preview:
Actions do indeed often speak louder than words. Saying and doing are two different things. In this section John stresses that the believer's walk is more important than his or her talk. He exhorts his readers who claim to be abiding in Christ to walk, or live, as Christ did (2:6). He follows his exhortation with examples of how such a walk manifests itself in everyday life.

The Commandment (2:7-8)

John's message concerning the need for the believer's walk to reflect his or her talk is not something never before declared by God. The recipients of John's letter had been told the truth earlier. They now needed a reminder.

Characteristic of John, he again summed up God's commandments in a single command. (For example, note 1 John 2:7. See further John 15:10, 12; 1 John 3:22-23; and 2 John 1:6). In the above texts the command from God for His people to love one another summarized Christ's commands.

Some of the oldest Greek manuscripts begin 2:7 with "Beloved" rather than "Brethren" as in the King James Version. Since the context is dealing with love, *beloved* does seem to be a better choice. The strong word for love in verse 7, *agapē*, in conjunction with *beloved*, connotes the idea of selflessness for the welfare of others. The same word appears in passages like John 3:16 and 1 John 4:8.

In 1 John 2:7 John is referring to "new" as it relates to quality. The Greek *kainos* is used rather than *neos*, which means new in point of time. "Commandment" here is from the same word as in verse 4. The Mosaic Law does not seem to be in view here but rather an exhortation or injunction. The "beginning" of time from which John says his readers had heard the command is no doubt a reference to the very beginning of the Christian era in general and to their non-Christian experience in particular (cf. John 13:34). Christ had given the apostles the command to love others as He loved them.

After describing the old commandment, John goes on to describe the "new commandment" (2:8). The commandment he was writing about was both old and new. It was *old* in the sense that it had been given before. They had heard it from the beginning of their Christian experience. It was *new* in the sense that it was "true in Him and in you" (v. 8). It was "in Him," in Christ. He loves His own, and His own are to love one another as He loves them (John 13:34). As Christ's people obey His command to them, they carry out a command that is characterized by truth in them and in the One Who gave the command and practiced it. This One, Christ, is here called "the true light [that] is already shining."

> At one time the darkness of paganism enshrouded the readers; now the genuine light is in them. Christ and the gospel have come into their hearts. More and more pagans are being brought from the darkness to the light; indeed, the darkness is thus passing away, the genuine light is shining (two progressive present tenses).[1]

"The darkness is passing away, and the true light is already shining" (1 John 2:8), John wrote. This is no doubt a part of the newness of the command in the first part of the verse. The new commandment to love, in other words, belongs not to the age of darkness but to the age of light that began with the coming of God's Son to earth to be our Savior. "The ancient systems of error, under which men hated each other, have passed away, and you are brought into the light of the true religion. Once you were in darkness, like others; now the light of the pure gospel shines around you, and that requires, as its distinguishing characteristic, *love*."[2]

The Positive Aspect of the Commandment (2:9–11)

First John 2:9–11 sounds much like 1:6–7. A hypothetical case is again presented: "The one who says . . ." (2:9). Both of the factual statements of 2:10–11 are similar to that of 1:7. John frequently sets forth a hypothetical case and then follows it with a straightforward statement of an actual occurrence.

The reference in 2:9 is to believers who claim to be "in the light" but hate fellow believers. No unsaved person is a spiritual brother, "his brother," to one who is born again. The affirmation then is clear and precise; a believer who hates another believer is not living in the true light manifested in the person of Christ. The opposite is true of such a person. Rather, he or she is "in the darkness until now," that is, has never experienced walking in the light. He or she is not living in this life in light of the day when all the spiritual darkness of this age will be done away and the righteousness of Christ will prevail.

A sharp contrast is set forth between love and hate in these verses (vv. 9–11). It is either one or the other. There seems to be no middle ground. "Hates" is in the present tense and therefore has to do with habitual, continuous animosity harbored in the heart.

The love in 2:10 is produced by the Holy Spirit in the believer's heart (Gal. 5:22). "Loves" is in the present tense and is the strong word for love (Greek, *agapē*). Self-sacrificial love with the best interests of others in mind is in view. Such behavior is not native to human nature; it can be manifested only by believers who are controlled by the Spirit of God.

The result of the demonstration of this kind of love follows (2:10): "There is no cause for stumbling in him." Both the person exercising this love and the one on whom it is bestowed are in view. "Cause for stumbling" is from the Greek *skandalon* and means tripped or trapped. Light illuminates his path to prevent him from stumbling (cf. John 11:9–10).

A contrastive particle introduces the result of hating one's brother (1 John 2:11). "But the one who hates his brother is in the darkness and walks in the darkness, and does not know where he is going because the darkness has blinded his eyes."

Two things are true of believers who hate a brother or sister in Christ. First, they are "in the darkness." This is living contrary to being in the light revealed and displayed by Christ. No matter what these persons claim about living or walking in the light, they are not doing so as long as they have hatred toward another believer. Second, the one John describes not only is "in the darkness," but "walks in the darkness" (v. 11). That is, such persons live outside of the spiritual light shining through and in God's Word.

Two consequences result from such behavior. First, the hating Christian "does not know where he is going" (v. 11). This threat seems to refer to God's future discipline of the sin of hating a child of God. Second, "the darkness has blinded his eyes." Living in a state of spiritual darkness in hatred hardens the heart and distorts one's perspective. In short, it creates more blindness, hardness, and hatred.

The Purpose of the Commandment (2:12–14)

In this section John gives reasons for his dwelling on the relation between the believer's fellowship with God and his or her walk or living. A difference in approach here is worth noting. Instead of "if we say" and "the one who says," he is now more personal: "I am writing" and "I have written."

Addressed are those called "little children" (2:12), "fathers" (v. 13), "young men" (v. 13), and again "children" (v. 13), perhaps indicating levels of spiritual maturity. Some find only three classes named, understanding "little children" and "children" to refer to the same group. Still others do not believe either three or four classes are being designated. Instead, all the titles refer to the entire readership from different points of view.[3] I understand John to be using four different descriptions of family members to describe the different levels of spiritual growth of those he addresses.

The "little children" of verse 12 may be translated "beloved children" or "little born ones." John may very well have led these to Christ himself. These are newborn babes in Christ. The Greek word used for them is *teknion*, highlighting their kinship while the word with the same translation, "children," in verse 14 is *paidion*, which carries the idea of responsibility. "Fathers" (2:13) refers to older men who had known the Lord for a long time. These were more mature in the faith. Some of them even may have seen Christ in the flesh. If so, they would be some of the eyewitnesses to which John refers. The "young men" (v. 13) were probably not as old in the faith as the fathers were, but they were nevertheless confirmed followers grounded in the things of the Lord. Finally, "children" (v. 13) seems clearly to refer to a different group from those in verse 12. The main reason is the different word used for them. These knew more than the little children of verse 12. They were a bit more mature yet not as mature as the fathers and young men were.

After spelling out who was being instructed, John turned to the reasons for his giving the instruction. The little children of verse 12 were instructed "because your sins are forgiven you for His name's sake." These newborns needed to know at the very beginning of their entrance into the family of God that the guilt and penalty of their sins had been removed from them. Christ bore their sins on the cross. They had been forgiven when they trusted the Savior, and the results or blessing of that past forgiveness remained with them (cf. Eph. 1:7).

John wrote to the fathers because they knew who was "from the beginning" (2:13). Because of their experience of walking with God, they gained knowledge of Him. They still needed more instruction. They had not yet arrived at the place where they no longer needed to grow in their Christian lives.

Young men (2:13) were on John's mind "because you are strong, and the word of God abides in you, and you have overcome the evil one" (v. 14). Throughout this section in which John explains why he is giving the instruction to these groups, the perfect tense of the verbs is used. This tense places emphasis on the permanent possession of these things. The young men were strong in the Lord and victorious in overcoming Satan and his wiles. Satan is "the evil one" (v. 13). This one

> is *ton ponēron*, the pernicious one. The Greek has two words for the idea of wickedness, *kakos*, evil in the abstract, and *ponēros*, evil in active opposition to the good. The *kakos* man is content to perish in his own corruption. The *ponēros* man seeks to drag everyone else down with him into his ultimate downfall. Satan is of the latter character, pernicious.[4]

John said of the children (2:13), "You know the Father." He states this as his reason for writing to them. As noted above, the word for children here is the Greek *paidion* in contrast to *teknia* in verse 1. The difference seems to be that in the case of *teknia* affection is stressed, whereas with *paidion* subordination/discipline is stressed.

> The thing to which John appeals here is the energy of those at this period of life, and it is proper at all times to make this the ground of appeal in addressing a church. It is right to call on those who are in the prime of life, and who are endowed with energy of character, to employ their talents in the service of the Lord Jesus, and to stand up as the open advocates of truth.[5]

In verse 14, John writes again this word of confirmation and encouragement to fathers and to young men. These *older* fathers had known Christ for some time, "from the beginning," and the young men had within them virility and strength. The word of God was abiding in them, and they had overcome the evil one, Satan.

The Negative Aspect of the Commandment (2:15–17)

In the preceding verses (2:12–14), John has given his readers reason to be confident that they have a wonderful position in Christ. Positionally they have already "overcome the evil one" (v. 14). They therefore have reason to rejoice in their riches of grace in Christ. Now he reminds these same people (vv. 15–17) that although they have overcome the evil one positionally, they still must contend with the evil one's anti-God philosophy on planet earth as they seek to live out their faith. This fierce one, this enemy of believers, is Satan.

Believers ever since John's day have had to face the same foe. "Do not love the world, nor the things in the world. If anyone loves the world, the love of the Father is not in him" (v. 15). The *world*, from *cosmos*, has several meanings in Scripture, especially in John's writings. The context determines which meaning it has. God brought the world into existence (John 1:10). God loved the world (John 3:16). Christ is said to be the *Light of the World* (John 1:9) and its Savior (John 4:42). Yet, the whole world (1 John 2:2) lies in the lap of the evil one, Satan (1 John 5:19).[6] Here in the passage under consideration (2:15) the cosmos is Satan's organized system, which is in direct opposition to God. It is expressed in the godless philosophy of humanism, the moral and spiritual system organized by Satan himself to draw humankind away from God.

John uses the strong word for love, *agape*, in his command (2:15). It is in the present tense and imperative mood; thus John seems to be calling for the cessation of that which was already going on. What he really was telling the little children then was "Stop loving the world." "With *the world* are joined 'the things in the world,' all, that is, which finds its proper sphere and fulfillment in a finite order and without God. 'To be in the world is the opposite of being in God.' . . . Whatever is treated as complete without reference to God is so far a rival to God."[7]

The command is followed by a very strong reason for it. "If anyone loves the world, the love of the Father is not in him" (2:15). John switches here from the second person to the third person. Instead of "if you love the world," he is saying, "If anyone loves the world." This could mean he is not referring to any of the believers but rather to others outside the family of God. Most likely, however, he is still addressing the same ones to whom he gave the command and is referring to anyone in that group loving the world.

The meaning of the "If anyone . . ." phrase then means that believers cannot love the world or the things in it that promote Satan's cause and love God at the same time. God and Satan's system are opposites and mutually exclusive. "This is surely what John means by the statement that 'the love of the Father is not in him.' Although the words *the love of the Father* could theoretically mean 'the father's love for' the person who loves the world, there is no good reason to take them that way."[8]

John next states the necessity of the negative command (2:16-17). The first reason he cites is the way of the world (v. 16): "For all that is in the world, the lust of the flesh and the lust of the eyes and the boastful pride of life, is not from the Father, but is from the world." "Lust" describes a craving desire. It is used of both good and bad things. In this context it obviously refers to desiring what is evil. "Flesh" is used variously in Scripture. In this setting it refers to the Adamic sin nature inherited from parents and still possessed by believers.

Evil, passionate desire is manifested in us through our eyes. The old sin nature manifests itself in this way; it finds expression often through what we see. The sin nature also manifests itself through the pride of life. "Pride" here means vain glory along with self-sufficiency and a false assurance. All the cosmos has to offer is not of the Father. Therefore, the world is not to be loved. Satan's anti-God system is under God's judgment. The world's prince has already been judged at Calvary.

The second reason the negative command was necessary was because Satan's world system is temporal (2:17). It will pass away. In fact, it is "passing away" now. The world is transient. The cosmos will no longer exist when God's purposes for it are realized (cf. 2:8). The earth, cursed because of humankind's sin, awaits purification and renewal (Rom. 8:19–23). The lusts of the world are also in the process of passing away.

Finally, "the one who does the will of God abides forever" (1 John 2:17). This reason seems to associate obedience—doing the will of God—with living or abiding forever, speaking of possessing eternal life.

Study Questions

1. Who is John addressing when he is writing to the fathers, the young men, the little children, and the children, in verses 12 and 13?

2. Who is the evil one?

3. How is the evil one overcome?

4. How does the apostle John view the world?

5. What is said about the world in the Gospel of John (1:9–10; 3:16; 4:42)?

6. How does the world exercise its sinful influence and moral tug upon humanity?

CHAPTER 5

Antichrists in the Last Hour
1 John 2:18-27

Preview:
Though one day in the future the true antichrist will arise, many throughout history have exhibited his heretical qualities. John alerts his audience to those present in his day and describes the heretical views to watch for, assuring the believers of their power of discernment since the Holy Spirit has anointed them.

The Reality of Antichrists (2:18-19)

The children to whom John wrote needed more understanding about their enemies. As their spiritual leader and guide, John warned them about false teachers and their denying that "Jesus is the Christ" (2:22), the Messiah. These deniers he calls antichrists. When they deny the Son, they also deny the Father. They could not, and no one else can, have the one without the other. To reject the one is to reject the other.

What did John mean by "the last hour" (2:18)? The definite article is absent before this phrase. This means the emphasis is not on a particular and definite time but rather on the characteristics of the time. Literally, John wrote, "Children, it is a last hour."

We may say, therefore, that "the last hour" of which John speaks is constituted as such not by its duration (which in any case is relative!) but by the fact that it is the last era of this present age and will be followed by the establishment of the kingdom of God on earth. As experienced by humanity it is a long period in duration, now more than two thousand years. But, as just mentioned, it is experienced differently by God.[1]

Albert Barnes says of "it is the last hour":

The closing period or dispensation; that dispensation in which the affairs of the world are ultimately to be wound up. The apostle does not, however, say that the end of the world would soon occur, nor does he intimate how long this dispensation would be. That period might continue through many ages or centuries.[2]

That which will characterize the Antichrist in the future was already true of the false teachers in John's day. This is why he writes of "many antichrists" (2:18). The future Antichrist is called by a number of names, such as the "man of lawlessness" (2 Thess. 2:3), the "beast . . . out of the abyss" (Rev. 11:7), and "the people of the prince who is to come" (Dan. 9:26).

Anti in *antichrists* can mean either substitution or opposition[3] or perhaps both/and. Contextually, the idea of opposition seems to characterize these described in John's day.

Those harassing the children to whom John wrote had at one time been a part of the group in the sense that they were numbered among them. Johnson's comments on 1 John 2:19 are most appropriate. "At one time they had all been part of the same community, but one group left ('they went out from us') and became secessionists. They are the false teachers whom the author now calls the 'antichrists.' A schism had occurred within the Johannine community, splitting it in two."[4]

This affirms, without any ambiguity or qualification, that if they had been true Christians they would have remained in the church; that is, they would not have apostatized. There could not be a more positive affirmation than that which is implied here, that those who are true Christians will continue to be such; or that the saints will not fall away from grace. John affirms it of these persons, that if they had truly been Christians they would never had departed from the church.[5]

The Recognition of Antichrists (2:20–23)

In sharp contrast to the antichrists, John's readers had "an anointing from the Holy One" (2:20). Anointing is from *chrisma*, which refers to a grace gift. They, in other words, had been anointed, set apart by the Holy Spirit when they trusted Christ as Savior, and therefore could discern truth from error (cf. v. 27). They had no reason to be shaken by the false teachers. "You do know" refers to the truth concerning Christ. John seems to be referring to those false teachers who claimed superior knowledge and believed that salvation was received through that knowledge (cf. v. 4) when he assures the anointed ones they "know." Not just some of the group knew truth; they *all* knew. Significantly, John used the word for *know* that refers to knowledge that was final rather than knowledge gained by experience. "The meaning cannot be that they knew all things pertaining to history, to science, to literature, and to the arts; but that, under the influence of the Holy Spirit, they had been made so thoroughly acquainted with the truths and duties of [Christianity], that they might be regarded as safe from the danger of fatal error."[6]

Though the children knew the truth, they still needed a reminder (2:21). They must have lacked some assurance as they were under the pressure of those who finally went out from them. John writes to encourage them, to strengthen them in the faith. The progression of John's argument is clear. "The children" (v. 18) "know" (v. 21). No lie is of the truth (v. 21). The liar he has in mind is the "one who denies that Jesus is the Christ" (v. 22). Such a person is "the antichrist." Further, all who deny the Son as fully God and fully man deny the Father also (v. 22). No one, John affirms, can have God the Father who denies the Son. "The one who confesses the Son has the Father also" (v. 23). The members of the holy Trinity are inseparable from each other. From eternity to eternity they have worked and will work in perfect harmony.

It appears that John stressed the relation of the Father and the Son to each other because the beginning of the Cerinthian form of the Gnostic heresy was being felt among the believers. Cerinthus, who was of Jewish ancestry, denied the miraculous conception of Jesus. He taught that after John baptized Jesus, *the Christ* came upon Jesus and stayed with Him while He performed His miracles. Near the end of Jesus' life on earth *the Christ* departed from Him.

John's Use of the Word "Antichrist" in His Epistles

As the actual person of the antichrist who "is coming" (1 John 2:18).

As individual heretics who had arisen and were propagating similar lies the future antichrist will spread (1 John 2:18).

As antichrist liars who denied that Jesus was the Christ and who also denied both the Father and the Son (1 John 2:22).

As evil men, who in "the spirit of the antichrist," do not confess that Jesus is from God (1 John 4:3).

As evil antichrist-like deceivers who did not acknowledge that Jesus Christ had come in the flesh (2 John 1:7).

The Refuge from the Antichrist's Teaching (2:24–27)

John next informs his readers, whom he has been assuring that they know the truth because of the anointing of the Spirit upon them, of their refuge from the false teaching around them (2:24–27). John's readers did not need to learn anything from the secessionists or revisionists. They were fully competent to give scriptural defense for the absolute deity and full humanity of the Lord Jesus Christ.

It is of great importance that the Greek pronoun *humeis*, "you," in verse 24 stands at the beginning of the sentence. This shows the contrast between John's readers and the false teachers he had just renounced.[7]

> One might have expected the emphasized "you" to be the agent in what follows; but the real agency is divine, for "what you have heard" implies divine revelation. The "you" are being asked to let the revelation be active in them. For that revelation (expressed comprehensively by a neuter) the author reaches back to "the beginning" of Jesus' self-revelation to his disciples, and also to the repetition of that revelation at "the beginning" of the audience's experience as Johannine Christians.[8]

The apostle encouraged his readers to hold fast to sound doctrine. They were to "abide" or remain in the truth they embraced when they trusted Christ. The Greek word for "abide" in 2:24, *menō*, has in it the idea of allowing the truth embraced to mature them and thus make them stable. The basis of their fellowship or abiding in Christ (John 15:4) was the truth they had already received.

The "this" of 1 John 2:25 may refer to the abiding communion or fellowship described in verse 24. Or it may refer to what follows—eternal life (v. 25). Both are grammatically possible and both stress that eternal life relates to and results from union with the Father and the Son. Those described by John as antichrists were doing everything in their power "to deceive" the believers to whom John wrote (v. 26).

Up to this point (vv. 24–25) the writer appealed to the external apostolic witness the little children "heard from the beginning" (v. 24). Now he turns to the internal witness of the Holy Spirit for confirmation of the true messages. The Spirit seals for them the message they received concerning Christ. As in verse 24, so again in verse 27, the pronoun *you* appears first in the Greek text. Sharp contrast is made again therefore between the antichrists and the little children. Also, the anointing refers to the person of the Holy Spirit (cf. v. 20) who is the believer's teacher. The personal pronoun *Him* could refer to either the Father or the Son. The Son, the Anointed One, and God the Father sent the Holy Spirit.

"You have no need for anyone to teach you" is John's way of reminding the little children that they have the Holy Spirit in them and are therefore not at the mercy of the antichrists, the false teachers. The phrase must not be taken to mean that John was setting aside the need for the teaching ministry of the Word whether in written or oral form (cf. Acts 13:1; Eph. 4:11). John himself was teaching them in this very epistle. They needed his instruction, and we need it too.

Study Questions

1. What does it mean to abide?

2. What did John mean by saying, "Even now many antichrists have arisen" (2:18)?

3. What does John mean when he tells his audience that this is the "last hour"?

4. What does it mean to be anointed?

5. John writes, "The one who confesses the Son has the Father also" (2:23). Cite supporting passages from the Gospel of John.

6. Why did John say, "You have no need for anyone to teach you" (2:27)? Was John denying the need for Bible teachers?

CHAPTER 6

Fellowship with the Lord and His Return
1 John 2:28–3:3

Preview:

In this section of his epistle, John reminds his readers of the hope they have of being caught up to be with the Lord forever. He stresses the relationship between their fellowship with Christ and His return for them in the rapture.

When the prophetic Scripture is interpreted in precisely the same literal way in which the rest of Scripture is interpreted, there are clearly two aspects or stages of Christ's return. First, Christ will come to catch away the church, His bride. He will meet the redeemed in the air (John 14:1–6; 1 Cor. 15:51–58; 1 Thess. 4:13–18)—"they will be caught up . . . to meet the Lord in the air" (1 Thess. 4:17)—and He will take them to be with Himself while the seven-year Tribulation takes place on earth (cf. Rev. 6–18). This coming we call the Rapture. When it occurs, all the saved of this age will be raised from the dead to meet the Lord in the air also. After the seven-year Tribulation, Christ will return to earth with His saints to establish His kingdom on earth. This is the Second Coming. The coming to which John called the attention of the little children to whom he wrote this letter is the first stage of Christ's return, or the Rapture. Scripture describes this as the blessed hope toward which believers are to look (Titus 2:13).

Preparation for the Lord's Return (2:28)

The believer's preparation for the Lord's return is stated in positive and negative terms. Positively, the little children were told to "abide in Him" (2:28). There is a shift here in John's instruction. He has already told them about the false teachers he calls antichrists and how to find refuge from their teaching. Now he gives his readers another assignment, which is to be carried out while they obey the earlier one. They and all of God's people are to abide in Christ while opposing false teaching and while looking for the return of Christ.

To "abide in Him" (2:28) means to be in fellowship with Christ. For believers this involves living a Christlike life. Christ Himself described it in His instruction to His disciples when He said, "Abide in Me" (John 15:4). To the same disciples He also said on the same occasion that like branches in the vine, believers are "in Me" (John 15:2). To *abide* in Christ speaks of *communion* with Him. To be *in* Christ speaks of *union* with Him. Earlier John pointed out that to abide in Christ involves a Christlike walk (cf. 1 John 2:6).

"When" (1 John 2:28) may also be translated "if." John uses the subjunctive mood. This construction does not mean that John was expressing doubt about the fact that Christ will appear. Rather, he was acknowledging that there is uncertainty as to the exact time of His appearing.[1] New Testament saints expected the Lord to come again in their lifetime. They believed in the imminent hope of Christ's return.

The doctrine of the Lord's return was part of the primitive apostolic faith. Paul used four words (in verbal or substantive form) to describe it—Christ's coming (Greek, *parousia*), His appearing (Greek, *phanerosis*), His *epiphany* (Greek, *epiphaneia*), and His revelation (Greek, *apokalupsis*). Of these John uses the first two in this verse (28). There is ample evidence in the papyri that at that time in the East the word was the usual expression for the visit of a king or emperor. *Parousia* means literally "presence," and the two words together imply that our Lord's return will involve the personal presence of one now absent, the visible appearing of one now unseen.[2]

To "have confidence and not shrink away from Him" (2:28) presents the negative side of being prepared for Christ's return. Most likely John had in mind the believer's appearance before the *bema*, the Judgment Seat of Christ (cf. Rom. 14:10–12; 1 Cor. 3:11–15; and 2 Cor. 5:10–11). After the Rapture all believers will appear at this *bema* to give an account to Christ Himself as to how they lived their Christian life. Did they build on wood, hay, and stubble or on gold, silver, and precious stones? Believers on that day will be ashamed to face Christ if they are out of fellowship with Him. This Judgment Seat of Christ is only for believers who will either receive rewards or lose them even though they themselves will be saved yet so as by fire. Unbelievers will not appear at the *bema*. They will appear at the Great White Throne Judgment (Rev. 20:11–15).

Occupation in View of the Lord's Return (2:29–3:1)

The righteous acts of believers reveal their relation to the Savior. "If you know that He is righteous, you know that everyone also who practices righteousness is born of Him" (2:29).

Two different Greek words are translated "know" in this verse. The first one has to do with knowledge that is certain and sure. It becomes the basis of knowledge that is experiential, which is the second *know*. The one who knows absolutely that He is righteous knows also experientially "that everyone . . . who practices righteousness is born of Him" (v. 29). The second *know* may be translated either as an indicative, in which case John simply would be declaring a fact, or an imperative, which would involve a charge or command. There are arguments in the context for both moods. It does seem fitting for John to use the imperative since he used it before—"abide" (2:28) and immediately after "See" (3:1). He is giving here a series of commands that also argue for the imperative.

Since it is Christ who will appear (2:28), grammatically He is also the One to whom the pronoun *Him* refers in 2:29. This makes for a unique expression used only here in the New Testament—"born of [Christ]"—rather than "born of God" or "born of the Spirit."

The Father's love for the believer is the motivation for being occupied with Him in view of Christ's return (3:1). The righteousness of God in Christ moved John to think of the Father's love showered on His children. "See how great a love the Father has bestowed upon us, that we should be called children of God." "See" is plural. All God's people need to stop whatever we are doing and take notice of our heavenly Father's love. It is a great love, unique, unusual, and superior to every other love we could experience. Glenn Barker writes, "See how great the gift of his love really is! Why he has identified us as being his very own children! And this is exactly what we have become through his acts. We have really been born of him. Clearly the author means to encourage his readers by reminding them of the grace of God they have received through the lavishness of God's own love."[3]

The believer's position in the family of God cannot be understood by the world (3:1). The unregenerate are blinded by Satan (2 Cor. 4:4). They do not have the spiritual equipment to understand spiritual things. The same spiritual blindness kept the Jewish leaders from knowing and receiving Christ when He was here: "It did not know Him" (1 John 3:1). He came to them, but they received Him not (John 1:11).

There is no greater motivation for Christian service in view of Christ's return than God's love for us.

Transformation at the Lord's Return (3:2)

John is here telling his readers about the same climactic event, the Rapture of the church, as Paul told the Corinthian believers (cf. 1 Cor. 15:51–54). The assertion by Paul, "we shall be changed" (v. 52), is restated by John: "When He appears, we shall be like Him, because we shall see Him just as He is" (1 John 3:2).

John assured his believing readers that "now we are children of God" (3:2). The believer's position in the family of God does not depend on his or her spiritual maturity. It depends solely on his or her relation to God through Jesus Christ. With that settled, John goes on to tell his audience what will be true of them when they see Christ. "We shall be like Him, because we shall see Him just as He is." This means the believer's physical body will be made in "conformity with the body of His glory" (Phil. 3:21). It means the mortal body will become immortal. The corrupt and decaying body will put on incorruption (cf. 1 Cor. 15:53–54). The believer will receive a glorified body when Christ appears (1 John 2:28) at the Rapture.

Sanctification in View of the Lord's Return (3:3)

The promise in 3:3 is that "everyone who has this hope fixed on [the Lord] purifies himself, just as He is pure. The ultimate triumph of the believer is here called his or her "hope." Every believer has this hope. The *hope* in verse 3 is a noun, not a verb. It is what we possess, not what we expect to get.

"Purifies" (v. 3) speaks of setting oneself apart for God. The need to not love the world (2:15), to practice righteousness (2:29), and to abide in Christ (3:6) all support the fact that progressive sanctification is in view in the word *purifies*. When the reality of the imminent return of Christ grips the believer's heart, he or she will be driven to God's Word for cleansing and purifying. The pattern here is the altogether pure One, Christ. Barker further states:

> All who have their hope in Jesus, i.e., their hope of being like him (3:2) when he appears (2:28), will also be committed to keeping themselves from sin. They will put away defilement; they will aim to be like him in purity and righteousness. Once more we have the pattern of the incarnate Jesus being held up as an example to believers (cf. 2:6; 3:7, 16; 4:17). Those who claim likeness to him must be conformed to his earthly life, even as they wait for his coming.[4]

Henry Alford adds:

> The man who purifies himself has this hope, resting upon God. This mere fact implies a will to purify himself, not out of, nor independent of, this

hope, but ever stirred up by, and accompanying it. So that the will is not his own, sprung out of his own nature, but the result of his Christian state, in which God also ministers to him the power to carry out that will in self-purification.[5]

Study Questions

1. What does John mean when he writes, "When He appears, we shall be like Him" (3:2)?

2. When Jesus returns, what will cause us to "shrink away from Him in shame at His coming" (2:28)?

3. Although it appears that unsaved people can do good works, are they truly practicing righteousness? If not, why not?

4. Since the world does not know us, how does it feel about us? Cite supporting passages from the Gospel of John.

5. How do we purify ourselves?

CHAPTER 7

Sins, the Savior, and the Sons of God
1 John 3:4–12

Preview:
John explains why those who are saved cannot continuously sin and why those who are unsaved can do nothing but continuously sin. These two groups are described respectively as the "children of God" and the "children of the devil." Both groups can do nothing but follow their respective master.

Sin and the Savior (3:4–5)

The true nature of sin is set forth in 3:4: "Everyone who practices sin also practices lawlessness; and sin is lawlessness." This is, of course, in direct contrast to the purity of Christ in 3:3. Law here must not be understood as referring simply to the Mosaic legal statutes. Sin was in the world long before Moses penned these statutes. Divine law in the broad sense is in view. Any infraction of any part of God's law is sin. Zane Hodges believes "iniquity" is a better translation of *anomia* than "lawlessness." All sin, he insists, is evil, wicked, and iniquitous.[1]

Christ, the Savior, gave Himself as the sacrifice for sin. "He appeared in order to take away sins" (3:5). There is absolutely no sin in Him. The pronoun *He* with "appeared" in verse 5 clearly has as its antecedent the "He" in verse 3, and that "He" goes back to Him who shall appear and transform all His own (v. 2). Both the first coming of Christ (v. 5) and His future coming in the clouds of glory for His own (v. 2) are incentives for holy living.

"Appeared" (3:5) is from the Greek *phaneroō* and is used several times in this context (cf. 2:28 and 3:2). Christ appeared at His first advent "to take away sins" (3:5). His forerunner, John the Baptist, declared He was the One "who takes away the sin of the world" (John 1:29). The plural "sins" is used in 1 John 3:5 and the singular "sin" in John 1:29. Taken together this tells us that the sacrifice of the Savior was in payment for both the sin nature and the actual individual acts of sin.

> The essential argument here is, that the whole work of Christ was designed to deliver us from the dominion of sin, not to furnish us the means of indulgence in it; and that, therefore, we should be deterred from it by all that Christ has done and suffered for us. He perverts the whole design of the coming of the Saviour who supposes that his work was in any degree designed to procure for his followers the indulgences of sin, or who so interprets the methods of his grace as to suppose that it is now lawful for him to indulge his guilty passions.[2]

Sin is foreign to the Son of God. "In Him there is no sin" (1 John 3:5). He did not and does not have a sin nature, and He did not and does not commit deeds of sin.

Sin and the Sons of God (3:6–12)

Evangelicals are greatly divided over the meaning of this passage, especially 3:6, 9. To help us arrive at the true meaning of this difficult section, we must first distinguish between the believer being "in Christ" and his or her "abiding" in Christ. John's use of "abides" (v. 6) is highly significant. In his gospel he used both phrases, "in Me," referring to *union* with Christ, and "abide in Me," referring to *communion* or fellowship with Christ (John 15:2, 4).

> The one who abides in Him is not here a spiritual Christian in contrast to a carnal Christian; this is a born-again person in contrast to one who is not saved. The born-again person is seen as one who habitually abides in Christ; that person does not habitually practice sin. This does not suggest that the believer never commits one single act of sin but he will not habitually live a life of sin. A sinful life does not mark a child of God.[3]

"No one who abides in Him sins," therefore speaks of the believer being in fellowship. When this is the case, the believer does not sin just as surely as when the child of God abides in Christ, he or she may ask for whatever he or she wishes "and it shall be done for you" (John 15:7).

John R. W. Stott lists seven answers that have been given in answer to the question, "What does John mean when he says the Christian abiding in Christ does not sin (1 John 3:6) and cannot sin (v. 9)?"

1. The sins that the believer cannot commit are restricted to notorious crimes. Distinction is often made between sins of omission and sins of commission.

2. The Christian cannot sin because what is sin for an unbeliever is not regarded as such for the believer.

3. Distinction is drawn between the old and new natures in the believer. The old nature continues to sin, but the new nature does not.

4. John in these verses is describing the ideal and the reality.

5. Among those who hold the previous view, some stress that it is really a relatively realistic view that John sets forth. In reality, not all Christians do abide in Christ.

6. For those who are truly born again it is impossible to willingly and willfully do what they know is forbidden by God.

7. The sins committed by Christians are not characteristic of him/her. They are exceptions, not the rule. When true Christians sin, they are grief-stricken and repent of such.[4]

Where does the truth lie? How are we to understand John's affirmations in 3:6 and 9 in relation to his equally strong affirmations in 1:8–10? I offer the following suggestions. First, the contexts both before and after 3:6 and 9 make it abundantly clear that believers can and do sin (1:7–10; 2:1; 5:16–17). Second, John's use of the present tense throughout this epistle and especially in 3:6 and 9, along with the stress on the word *abiding* must not be summarily set aside as insignificant.[5]

Even though Hodges rejects the use of the Greek present tense in 3:6 and 9 as the solution to the apparent contradiction between 1:8 and 3:6 and 9, he does not believe a believer can be completely free from sin: "To be sure, no Christian can ever claim (in this life) to be experientially completely free from sin, as 1:8 makes emphatically clear."[6] He does not believe abiding in Christ is contaminated by the presence of sin in another area of our lives. He holds that when a believer abides in Christ, that obedience is what God recognizes, and any sin in us is cleansed away in accordance with 1:7. "No one who sins has seen Him or knows Him" (3:6) is an additional troubling phrase. "The present perfect [used here] does not imply a 'never' unless the context requires it. So I may say, 'I have not finished my homework,' implying the homework for that particular day. There is no implication that I have never at any time completed my homework. . . . John simply means that when a person sins, at that point he has acted in blindness and ignorance of God."[7]

My own understanding of 3:6 and 9 has been simply stated in the *Ryrie Study Bible* notes on these verses: "The lifestyle of the believer who keeps God's commands (abides) will be obedience, not sin. The lifestyle of the one who keeps on sinning demonstrates that he does not know God. . . . Habitual actions indicate one's character."[8]

John did not want the little children or "little born ones" to whom he wrote to be deceived by anyone (3:7). Very likely the deceivers he had in mind were the same ones he called antichrists and liars earlier (2:18, 22). "The one who practices righteousness is righteous, just as He is righteous" (3:7 cf. 2:29). Good works are the natural result of faith in Christ. Life, including divine life, cannot be hidden very long. When sinners are united to the One who possesses pristine purity, they will sooner or later strive for purity in their lives. The "righteous" One in 3:7 is the "pure" One of 3:3. We must be sure to understand John correctly. The doing of *righteous* deeds does not make one righteous. The unrighteous are made righteous by grace alone through faith alone in Christ alone.

> The Gnostic false teachers were seeking to deceive the saints, but their high profession and low living were contrary to each other. They claimed that, although they were living lawless lives, nevertheless because of their superior knowledge this was righteous but of course "righteous without a determination to practice righteousness." John would have the saints to know that profession and practice must correspond.[9]

The Greek word translated "practices" in 3:8 and 9 is the common one for "to do," *poieō*. It is in the present tense in both instances. In direct contrast to the one described in verse 7 who "practices righteousness" (from the same verb) and by so doing gives evidence that he or she has been declared righteous by God is the one in verse 8 who practices sin and thus gives evidence of being "of the devil."

Up to this point John has said much about sin and antichrists. This is the first time (3:8), however, he has brought Satan into the epistle. In doing this he highlights the true source from which both sin and teaching of the antichrists come. Sin has no relation to God; it is completely associated with the devil. Therefore, sin, whether in the life of the believer or the unbeliever, originates with Satan. He is the one who committed the first sin in the universe.

"The Son of God appeared for this purpose, that He might destroy the works of the devil" (3:8 cf. 3:5). Even before Jesus' death, He declared the certainty of His defeat of Satan (cf. John 16:11). The Savior's death rendered the works of the devil inoperative for the believer. Satan has been judged. He is a defeated foe. In God's timing Satan's sentence will be carried out by his being cast into the eternal lake of fire.

To be "born of God" (3:9) is to partake of the divine nature (cf. 2 Pet. 1:4). In 1 John 2:29 John used similar terminology, "born of Him" (cf. 1 John 4:7; 5:1, 4, 18; John 1:13; 3:3, 5). I have already commented above on 1 John 3:6 and 9 in relation to 1 John 1:7–10. A few additional explanations, however, are in order.

Here in 1 John 3:9 additional things are included in the affirmation. First, instead of "abides in Him" (v. 6), verse 9 has "born of God." Second, "sins" (v. 6) is replaced with "practices sin" (v. 9). Third, verse 6 has "no one who abides in Him sins," whereas, verse 9 says that it is because God's "seed abides in him" that one does not practice sin. God's *seed* (3:9) refers most likely to the new nature imparted to the believing sinner at the time of salvation. A. T. Robertson quoting Marvin C. Vincent calls it *the divine principle of life*.[10] Robertson also considers "and he cannot sin" (v. 9) a wrong translation because it means the believer cannot commit sin

> . . . as if it were *Kai ou dunatai harmartein* or *hamartesai* (second aorist or first aorist active infinitive). The present active infinitive *hamartanein* can only mean "and he cannot go on sinning," as is true of *hamartanei* in verse 8 and *hamartanon* in verse 6. For the aorist subjunctive to commit a sin see *hamartate* and *hamartei* in 2:1. A great deal of false theology has grown out of a misunderstanding of the tense of *hamartanein* here. Paul has precisely John's idea in Rom. 6:1 *hamartiai* . . . in contrast with *hamartesomen* in Rom. 6:15.[11]

Stephen Smalley's comments on the "and he cannot sin" phrase (3:9) coincide with Robertson's above.

> John concludes this section by reminding his readers that the true child of God is (like the Father himself) opposed to sin. Whereas the determined sinner (the heretic in John's church, perhaps, as opposed to the orthodox Christian) belongs to the devil (v. 8), the spiritually reborn believer, being a member of God's family, *cannot as a settled policy* [italics mine] act lawlessly (cf. v. 4). In other words, we reproduce in our lives a "family" likeness depending upon our spiritual parentage; and those who are "born of God" do not sin (cf. vv. 7, 8, 10).[12]

Kenneth Wuest insists that the present infinitive form at the end of 1 John 3:9, as it always does, speaks of continuous, habitual action, never the mere fact of the action. "The aorist infinitive which refers to the fact of the action, may be used at will if the writer wishes to speak of the mere fact without reference to details."[13]

"By this the children of God and the children of the devil are obvious: anyone who does not practice righteousness is not of God, nor the one who does not love his brother" (3:10). Love of one's brother and practicing righteousness are acid tests as to which family one is in—God's or the devil's. This seems to be what John is saying in 5:10. From this verse on to the end of the epistle, there are no more specific references to *righteousness*. This verse then seems to be a link between what has preceded it and what follows. Love, which of course is the outworking of righteousness, is the new theme.

> "By this" refers back to what has gone before, the doing or not doing of righteousness, but the statement is so placed between the preceding verses concerning righteousness and those that follow concerning love. This chapter . . . deals with the features of righteousness and love showing our resemblance to our Father. Here the two characteristics are brought together and the existence of righteousness and love on the one hand shows that one is the child of God, and the existence of lawlessness and hate on the other hand is the evidence of one being a child of the devil.[14]

"Not of God" (v. 10) parallels "of the devil" (v. 8) in structure. "Of the devil" means the person so characterized was energized by the devil. By the same token, "not of God" (v. 10) means God is not the source from which the action originates. Both phrases make clear that God is not pleased with the believer who does not practice righteousness and does not love his brother (vv. 8, 10).

Christ commanded us to "love one another" (John 13:34). When we do not do so, we violate His command, which means we sin. Only believers were given this command. John's readers had been told this was their responsibility "from the beginning" (1 John 3:11). Early in their Christian experience they were so instructed. Christ Jesus came into the world to display God's love for humankind. It follows then that all who are Christ's should love one another.

The wicked deed of Cain must have come as a stinging reminder to John's readers: "Not as Cain, who was of the evil one, and slew his brother. And for what reason did he slay him? Because his deeds were evil, and his brother's were righteous" (3:12). The reason John brought up this incident was doubtless to set forth a case in point where one's evil works demonstrated that he was "of the evil one." Cain, in other words, by his lifestyle, his wicked works, gave evidence to the fact that he was of the devil (cf. v. 8).

"Evil one" is the translation of a word that means actively evil, opposed to all that is good. The word *pernicious* would be a good translation of it. "Slew" (v. 12) describes something worse than "killed." In classical Greek the word was used to describe the way victims were prepared for sacrifice—by cutting the throat (cf. Gen. 4:4–5, 8–10).

Study Questions

1. What was the main task of the Lord Jesus when He first came to earth?

2. How is sin foreign to the Son of God?

3. What does John mean when he writes that believers cannot sin?

4. How are these verses reconciled by the clear and abundant evidence that believers do indeed sin (1:7–10; 2:1; 5:16–17)?

5. How do Ryrie and Lightner explain verses 6 and 9 (See p. 71)?

6. In what way does the believer who has been born of God (3:9) partake of the divine nature (cf. 2 Pet. 1:4)?

7. How does Smalley explain verse 9 (see p. 73)?

CHAPTER 8

Hate and Love
1 John 3:13-24

Preview:

John continues his distinctions between the saved and unsaved, describing the relation of the two as being one of love and hate. By virtue of their salvation in Christ, those who are saved can now truly love and should express that love for their brethren in tangible ways, as well as showing their love to God by obeying His commandments. Those who are unsaved cannot truly love and, moreover, will hate those who can love because of their relationship with Jesus Christ.

Hatred from the World (3:13)

The "brethren" were reminded that sometimes brothers hate each other (3:12). Such behavior is totally inconsistent with both the character of God and His command. Now John tells them they were not to be surprised when they would be hated by the world. "Do not marvel, brethren, if the world hates you" (v. 13). There is room to "marvel," to be surprised, when brother hates brother, but hatred from the world toward all who name His name should be expected.

This is the first and only time John calls his readers "brethren" (v. 13). B. F. Westcott defines the term and distinguishes it from other descriptions.

The three forms which St. John borrows from the family to express Christian relations preserve each their proper meaning. "Brethren" expresses the idea of Christian equality in virtue of the common life:

"Children (*teknia*) that of spiritual dependence in the order of the new life with the prospect of growth: "Little ones" (*paidia*) that of subordination and immaturity. In contrast with these "Beloved" is simply the personal manifestation of feeling.[1]

Assurance of Eternal Life (3:14-18)

The pronoun *we* (3:14) is in the emphatic position placing contrast between what the *cosmos* headed by the devil does (v. 13) and what the child of God knows. It is significant to note the repetition of the phrase "we know" in this context (cf. vv. 14, 16, 19, 24, and "you know" in v. 15). Throughout the entire epistle—especially here in chapter 3—there is an emphasis on assurance.

John makes love for the brethren a sign of life and hate and murder signs of death. Love for the brethren is not the ground of eternal life but the result of the possession of life. "He who does not [practice (based on the present tense)] love abides in death" (v. 14), meaning such a one shows no signs of being a child of God.[2]

In Cain's case, hate resulted in murder (v. 12). One who habitually hates is a murderer at heart (v. 15), a potential murderer. Such a one does not have "eternal life abiding in him" (v. 15). Just as light is the opposite of darkness, so life is the opposite of death.

God's love for the lost was demonstrated climactically at Calvary. John reminded his readers of this (v. 16). Christ's was a sacrificial love. "He laid down His life for us" speaks clearly of the substitutionary work of Christ on the cross. Believers are all related to Christ and to each other, and therefore they too ought to love one another actively and sacrificially.

There is further evidence of the kind of love John was calling for from his readers, whom he identifies as "little children" (v. 18). The contrastive particle *but* (v. 17) introduces a contrast with what was said in verse 16. The contrast describes what it means to lay down one's life for the brethren. It means showing definite interest and lending a helping hand to those in need.

Most specifically, when a believer has the means to help those believers in need but instead of helping "closes his heart against him," there is evidence that God's love is certainly not at that time abiding in him (v. 17). John asks the question, "How does the love of God abide in him?" The answer is not given, but it is self-evident. James asked and left unanswered the same question (cf. James 2:15-16).

Assurance in Prayer (3:19–24)

Before introducing the subject of prayer, John addresses the matter of the troubled guilt-ridden heart of the believer. This issue stems from the searching question raised in 3:17: "How does the love of God abide in him?" This question was raised concerning one who is able to help those in need but does not help them. All honest believers would admit that often they feel they have not done enough or perhaps that what was done was not a genuine expression of love. Have we really truly loved? Have we really acted and participated in the truth? Are we "of the truth"?

As he has done throughout this section, John emphasizes assurance. Security and assurance must always be kept distinct. The former is God's business. He provides security Himself. Assurance comes to the secure saint as a result of trusting and resting in the security God provides. No matter what our heart—the seat of our emotions—tells us, God knows our true motive and assures us we have done what He wants us to do and is pleased with us.

God knows all things, including our hearts, and is greater than our doubting heart (v. 20). Our great all-knowing God is also loving, gracious, and compassionate. When our heart does not condemn us, we have confidence before God (v. 21). When the heart condemns, we have little or no confidence before God.

John, it must be kept in mind, is not describing a sinless Christian in the phrase "if our heart does not condemn us." Rather, the believer who is in fellowship with God knows of no unconfessed sin and is living in the power of the Holy Spirit. Each child of God needs to take periodic inventory of his or her walk with God. Such self-analysis is needed in preparation for prayer (vv. 19–21).

> Peter had declared he would lay down his life for the Lord, and had failed to fulfil his pledge. Thus John is teaching here that if we have been characterised by this self-sacrificing love and we have expressed that love truly to our brother in his need, then by that we have evidence that we are of the truth and our hearts will be assured (convinced, persuaded) of that fact in His presence: "And shall assure our hearts before him". The order in the original is "and before Him we shall assure our hearts".[3]

The practice of prayer (3:22, 24) follows the instructions about the heart attitude when expressing love for the brethren. "And whatever we ask we receive from Him, because we keep His commandments and do the things that are pleasing in His sight. And this is His commandment, that we believe in the name of His Son Jesus Christ, and love one another, just as He commanded us" (vv. 22–23).

In the previous section John has already set forth one prerequisite to answered prayer—an uncondemning heart that results in confidence toward God (v. 21). Two more are added to this one in verse 22: (1) keeping God's commandments and (2) doing those things that please Him. "Whatever we ask we receive from Him" (v. 22) must be understood in its context. The promise is qualified by the surrounding conditions the prayer must meet. When these are met, the requests will be garnished by the will of God. The best example of praying with the will of God in focus is the Lord Himself: " . . . remove this cup from Me; yet not what I will, but what Thou wilt" (Mark 14:36).

Further description of the commandments (1 John 3:22) is given in v. 23. The "beloved" (v. 21) to whom John wrote had already trusted Jesus Christ as their personal Savior. Now they are challenged to believe and entrust their lives to the same Savior. Verse 23 is a summary of verses 19 through 22. The singular "commandment" is used in verse 23. Faith and love are the two inseparables that form the one commandment. The word *on* is not in the Greek text. The commandment therefore is "believe in the name of His Son." "Believing the name of God's Son is a prerequisite, and an essential component, of love for one another."[4]

Obedience to God's Word brings assurance, or confirmation, of fellowship with Him. The believer is here (v. 24) said to be abiding in God and God in the believer. The Holy Spirit is mentioned in verse 24 for the first time in the epistle. He is referred to several times in the remainder of the book. John, like Paul, affirmed that the Holy Spirit of God gives assurance to the believing and obeying heart (3:24 cf. Rom. 8:16).

Study Questions

1. If the world "abides in death" can it truly love?

2. What is the ultimate expression of love?

3. What tangible expressions of love does John state in this section?

4. What does it mean that our hearts may "condemn us"?

5. Are *assurance* and *security* the same thing?

6. According to this section, with which members of the Godhead are we abiding?

CHAPTER 9

Exhortations to the Beloved
1 John 4:1–10

Preview:
In this section John touches on a number of subjects he introduced earlier. False teachers and their evil words and works were discussed before (cf. 2:18–27). The assurance the children of God may have surfaced several times before. The redemptive work of Christ was brought forth earlier also (cf. 2:1–2; 3:5, 8, 16). And the same is true of the love of God (cf. 2:5, 15; 3:1, 16). From the very beginning of the epistle, John encouraged believers to love one another, and he does it again here (cf. 2:10; 3:10, 11, 14, 18). The tender term beloved *is used of John's readers twice in 4:1–10. Each time it introduces a new section.*

Test the Spirits (4:1–6)

In these first six verses John expounds on the thought he introduced in 3:23 and 24. In 3:23 John told his readers to "believe in the name of [God's] Son Jesus Christ." Now he tells them what not to believe (4:1). Likewise, the Holy Spirit was introduced as God's gift to the believer (3:24). Here they are told how to know the teaching of the Spirit of God from that of false spirits (4:1–2).

John's exhortation is very direct: "Beloved, do not believe every spirit" (4:1). Very likely John chose to address his readers with the tender "beloved" to soften his terse exhortation. The exhortation is twofold (one part negative and the other positive)—"do not believe" and "test the spirits." The prominent inroads of Gnostic thinking had apparently already begun to influence John's readers. The incipient seeds of Gnosticism had been sown and had begun to sprout. This was a serious perversion of Christ and therefore of

Christianity. It was a mixture of Jewish and Christian doctrines as well as heathen beliefs with a highly speculative emphasis. The entire system of Gnosticism was built on the opposites and antagonism between matter and spirit. Gnostics believed these two opposites were reconciled through spirit beings called "aeons." Gnosticism denied the incarnation of Christ and made a difference between Jesus and Christ.

Whether early Gnostics or other secessionists[1] or revisionists[2] were responsible for the false teaching John countered here (4:1–6) is really not the most important thing. What is very important is that John exhorted his little children, his beloved ones, to stop believing every spirit and teaching. Some in his audience had already begun to believe the false teachers, so the Spirit of God through John told them to *stop believing* false teaching about Christ.

Instead of believing every spirit, John's readers should "test the spirits" to see whether they are from God (4:1). "Spirits" in this phrase refers to the false teaching being presented by the false teachers. The two can hardly be separated (cf. 1 Tim. 4:1). The testing, proving, or trying of the spirits needed to be done to determine error from truth. What was needed then is still needed today by God's people. "Many false prophets" had gone out into the world in John's day (4:1). The verb translated "have gone out" is in the perfect tense, implying that they had already established themselves among the people. Many have gone and are going out still in our own day. Just as the true Holy Spirit of God had spoken through the true prophets of God (2 Pet. 1:21), so the false spirits were speaking through the false prophets.

The way to determine the true from the false is clearly stated. Does the teaching affirm the incarnation of Christ? If it does, it is of God (4:2). John's use of the name Jesus Christ here is highly significant. The title speaks of both our Lord's genuine humanity and His absolute deity. The false teachings being circulated among the readers denied both of these. In John's day the earmark of the false teaching he was opposing was a denial of Christ's true humanity. The teaching that denied that Christ was both God and man was not of God but instead had its source in Satan. Such teaching was not from God but was of "the spirit of the antichrist" (4:3; cf. 2:18–25).

Many of the best MSS omit "Christ come in the flesh" from this verse but it is obviously the meaning which John wishes to convey. Those that confess not are said to be "not of God". It is therefore a simple thing to try the spirits whether they are of God. "This is the spirit of the antichrist, whereof ye have heard that it cometh; and now it is in the world already" (RV). The antichrist has not yet come—he will in his own time—but the antichristian nature and attitude is already in the world. The word "already" suggests that something more is expected to follow. See "the mystery of lawlessness doth already work . . . then shall be revealed the lawless one" (2 Thess. 2:7,8 RV).[3]

The "little children" (4:4) needed encouragement and reassurance. Because of their relation to God, they were qualified to "test the spirits" (v. 1). In verses 4–6 John moves from the exhortation to determine truth from error to a contrast between the false teachers—the spirit of antichrist—and the little children. The false teachers, or antichrists, are "from the world" (v. 5). That is why they speak as though from the world and are heard and received by the world.

By sharp contrast, John and the little children are "from God" (4:6). Satan and demonic forces speak through all the false teachers; *"they are from the world"* (v. 5). Believers all have spiritual endowments from God from which they can and should draw for victory and power to receive and proclaim the truth. The contrast between being "from God" (v. 4) and being "from the world" (v. 5) is striking. These phrases are descriptive of the sources from which the little children and the false teachers derive their strength and support. John gave great assurance to the little children when he said the One in them—the Godhead—was greater than the one in the world—Satan (v. 4).

Verses 5 and 6 describe the unholy union between the false teachers and the world in contrast to the holy union between believers and God. Because of the believers' union with God, there is no need for them to be led into the spirit of error by Satan and his demons.

Love One Another (4:7–10)

There does not seem to be a clear connection between verses 7–10 and the ones immediately preceding. After John urges believers to test the spirits, he abruptly switches gears and talks about the need to love one another. Upon closer examination, however, we find that the two sections are vitally connected to each other.

The little children are related to God; they are from God (vv. 2, 4, 6), who is love (v. 8). Furthermore, they are born of God (v. 7), who is love. He made the first move toward the sinner (4:9–10). It follows therefore that our position and practice in the family of God in contrast to those outside the family are because of His boundless, matchless love and grace (3:16).

The exhortation to love one another (4:7) is clear enough. Likewise is the reason for the exhortation, for love is of God (vv. 7, 8). The strong word for love, *agape*, is used here. Also, the exhortation "let us love" and the explanation "everyone who loves," are both in the present tense stressing continuous action—the practice of love.

It would appear at first sight to be an abrupt change from a somewhat painful subject to that which is far more pleasing to the reader. It is a transition from "the spirit of error" to loving one another; yet there is a connection. John has mentioned the Spirit of truth (v. 6) and surely the love of God is shed abroad in our hearts by the Holy Ghost. We have been born of the Spirit and thus have become the children of God. Therefore we ought to love one another. The spirit of error evidences itself in those who are of the world and they possess the opposite features, "Marvel not, my brethren, if the world hate you" (3:13).[4]

Again John draws a contrast with those who do not love. He uses the present tense again in 4:8: "The one who does not love does not know God." Interestingly, "know" (v. 8) is not in the present tense but is in the aorist, laying stress upon a specific, completed action in the past. Evangelical Greek scholars understand this phenomenon—*love*, present tense; *know*, aorist—differently and therefore translate it differently. Kenneth Wuest translates it, "did not know God."[5] He then adds, "Vincent says, 'He never knew.' Smith translates, 'did not get to know.'"[6] A. T. Robertson translates it, "has no acquaintance with God, never did get acquainted with him."[7]

Note that the two terms *God* and *love* in 4:8 are not interchangeable. God is love, but love is not God. The definite article appearing with *God* and not with *love* prohibits the interchange.

The divine example of love is set forth in 4:9–10. John shows how God demonstrated His love by His Son at Calvary. The teaching of 3:16 is repeated here. God not only exhorts His children to love one another; He demonstrated His own love and gave His children an example to follow. The stress is on Christ's incarnation as a manifestation of God's love (4:9 cf. 3:5). Further description of God's love is seen in the cross. God sent His Son to be the "propitiation for our sins" (4:10). *Propitiation* carries the meaning of satisfaction. The work of the Lord Jesus Christ on the cross is a complete satisfaction of the offended righteousness of God. God the Father is satisfied with the finished work of His Son. He paid it all (cf. 2:2). "He loves us and sent His Son to be the propitiation for our sins. Our sins had offended a holy God and we therefore deserved His righteous wrath. But the same God holy and righteous against whom we had sinned and whose wrath must be appeased, in amazing love sent His own Son—provided Him as a propitiation, from His own bosom."[8]

Study Questions

1. What "spirits" is John referring to in verse 1?
2. How does the believer in Christ *test* the spirits?

3. What forces are at work in the doctrines of the false teachers?

4. What kind of contrast is John making when he writes about being "from God" and being "from the world"?

5. What does it mean that "God is love"?

6. In order to truly love someone is it necessary for that person to love us in return?

CHAPTER 10

Union with God and Unity among the Brethren
1 John 4:11-21

Preview:
John was reminded of the tremendous responsibility God's boundless love for His own brings to each one who experiences that love. In his gospel, John wrote of the believer's union with Christ, God the Son (John 15). Here he describes the union the child of God has with God the Father.

Union with God (4:11-19)

For the third time in the epistle the redeemed of the Lord are called "beloved" (4:11 cf. vv. 1, 7). The connecting link between the first part of chapter 4 and the last part is found in verses 11 and 12. "If God so loved us" (v. 11) is a condition stated in the first class in the Greek. The meaning, therefore, is that it is assumed to be true and could be translated "Since God so loved us." God the Father and God the Son extended sacrificial love at Calvary (cf. v. 9). In response, the redeemed "ought" (v. 11) to love one another. As is often the case in this epistle, this exhortation is in the present tense, indicating that this love should be continuous, ongoing.

"No one has beheld God at any time; if we love one another, God abides in us, and His love is perfected in us" (4:12). The opening words of this verse are very much like John 1:18. "God" is in the emphatic position in the Greek in both references. The verbs, however, are different. "In John 1:18 the thought is of the vision which might be the foundation of revelation. Here the thought is of the continuous beholding which answers to abiding fellowship."[1]

The nature or essence of God is stressed since there is no definite article before the word *God*. This is what no one has ever seen. God in His essence is invisible though real and near to the believer. He abides in the believer (4:12). Two things, John says, are true of the one who continually manifests genuine love for others—God abides in that one and so does His love. Loving others does not bring about God's presence and His love; it is the other way around: The habitual showing of God's love to others demonstrates the reality of one's relationship with God. "His love is perfected in us" (v. 12). This does not refer to God's acts of love or the believer's acts of love toward God. Rather, the reference is to the love that God is in His very nature. "Perfected" means completed or accomplished.

John's Use of the Greek Word Telios (Perfect, Mature, Complete) and Related Words

Christ completed His work on the cross as given to Him by His Father (John 4:34; 5:36; 17:4).

Christ loved His disciples unto the end (John 13:1).

Christ's suffering and thirst on the cross fulfilled prophecy (John 19:28).

Jesus said "It is finished" (John 19:30).

By keeping God's word, the believer is matured by God's love (1 John 2:5).

God's love itself is said to perfect (mature) the believer (1 John 4:12, 17, 18).

Perfect (mature) love casts out fear (1 John 4:18).

The false teachers John referred to in 4:2–3 did not believe the physical death of Jesus was in fact the death of God's Son. Therefore, that death could not be the model for believers to follow. John, however, makes very clear that there can be no real Christian love shown to others that is not based on and modeled after the love God expressed at Calvary.

Not only is God at home in the believer, the believer is also in God (v. 13). What follows in verses 13–16 are evidences and assurances that this vital union between the believer and God is really true.

First, God "has given us of His Spirit" (v. 13). Experiential knowledge is in view here from the word *know* in the first part of verse 13. This work of the Holy

Spirit in the heart of the believer brings assurance of union with God. The Spirit provides confirmation to the child of God subjectively through the objective Word of God that he or she is God's possession (cf. John 14:16–17; 1 Cor. 6:19).

Second, in John's day it was a capital offense to ascribe the title *Savior of the world* to anyone other than the Roman emperor, who was also worshiped. "We have beheld and bear witness that the Father has sent the Son" (1 John 4:14) is reflective of 1:2. The *we* refers to John and the whole apostolic witness. It is in the emphatic position and doubtless includes the little children, John's readers. "In other words, the visible manifestation of eternal life through Christian love, so that this life can be seen in that love, is an enormously effective way to testify about the Saviorhood of Christ."[2]

> This assurance gives us the confidence, as we see in the future the certainty of a day of judgment for those who are not born again, that we shall not come into condemnation, we shall not be at the great white throne judgment, we have already passed from death unto life. Thus we have a double assurance because we find in ourselves the evidence of divine life. Loving the brethren "we know that we have passed from death unto life" (3:14) and we have confidence relative to the Day of Judgment (4:17).[3]

Third, another evidence of the believer's union with God is stated in verse 15. "Whoever confesses that Jesus is the Son of God, God abides in him, and he in God." To *confess* means to agree with or speak the same thing. The aorist tense used with the verb speaks of a definite act in the past at a particular point in time. In context here the confession referred to is the full deity of Christ. One who confesses to Christ's absolute deity is at the same time accepting His demands upon him. The confession, therefore, brings responsibility to obey His commands since He is God. A. T. Robertson stated it well: "This confession of the deity of Jesus Christ implies surrender and obedience also, not mere lip service (cf. 1 Cor. 12:3; Rom. 10:6–12). This confession is proof (if genuine) of the fellowship with God (1:3f; 3:24)."[4]

Finally, there is a final evidence/assurance that the union of God and the believer is really true. John states it this way: "We have come to know and have believed the love which God has for us. God is love" (1 John 4:16). God's love (cf. v. 8) for His own explains His union with each of His children and how each is united with God.

The verbs *know* and *believed* (4:16) are both in the perfect Greek tense. This lays stress upon a completed act with abiding results (cf. John 6:69). The opening words of verse 17 refer back to the close of 1 John 4:16: "The one who abides in love abides in God, and God abides in him." The indwelling of God and His love in the believer results in God's love being "perfected with us" (v. 17). The love referred to here is the love that God is in His essence. It is that which is produced in us by the Holy Spirit and brought to perfection or completion in us.

> John writes not of "the love that God hath for us", rather of the love God hath *in* us. What God hath done for us is the expression of His love in sending His own Son, but what He has done in us means far more. His love has been poured into us, shed abroad in our hearts by the Holy Spirit and from us flows out to others. "He that believeth on me, as the scripture hath said, out of his belly shall flow rivers of living water. (But this spake he of the Spirit, which they that believe on him should receive: for the Holy Ghost was not yet given; because that Jesus was not yet glorified)" (John 7:38,39). That same love now dwells in all God's people. We know that God is in essence love, and he that abideth in love does therefore abide in God and the God who is love abides in him. "Since God, who is love, indwells the believer, the believer must and will love his fellow believers. Thus love for the family of God is a vital test of one's salvation" (Burdick).[5]

The union of the believer and God guarantees that there will be no fear or lack of confidence when the believer appears at the *bema*, the Judgment Seat of Christ (1 Cor. 3:12–15). John explains why this is true: "As He is, so also are we in this world" (1 John 4:17). The believer is clothed with the righteousness of Christ and is a partaker of the divine nature. This new position of the sinner saved by God's grace removes all basis for fear of Him. Surely we will regret that we have not done more for God's glory, but God will not condemn anyone there as He will all who appear at the Great White Throne Judgment (Rev. 20:11–15). Only dispensationalists distinguish between these two future judgments as they do between the rapture and the second coming of Christ to the earth and between the time of the resurrection of the just and the unjust.

John writes in 1 John 4:18 that the dread of someone who mistreats or is a criminal. "There is no fear in love; but perfect love casts out fear." To be sure, believers are to have a godly fear and reverence (1 Pet. 1:17). Here, however, John means that God's love in the human heart removes the dread and makes the person bold. The perfect love of God casts out dreadful fear. The terror of God and His judgment is replaced by God's perfect love in the heart of His child. "There is no place for fear on our part in connection with the love of God for us. This love has removed all our sins ([1 John] 1:9; 2:1–2; 4:10); what is there left to make us afraid?"[6]

Fear involves punishment because that is what it brings to the human heart. The believer who fears to stand before God has not had love perfected, or completed, in his or her heart and life (4:18). God's love in such a person has not been fully appropriated. Those who rebel against God and His Word will have such a fear. This love of God must be appropriated by faith.

"We love, because He first loved us" (4:19). The grammatical construction of the phrase "we love" allows for two possible meanings. It may either be taken as translated above or as subjunctive, "let us love." The context lends support to both possibilities. The believer's love for God seems to be assumed in the context, and this makes "we love" the better of the two possibilities.

Unity among God's People (4:20-21)

John moves from his emphasis on the union between God and His children to what should be the natural corollary—the practical result of that union. Brothers and sisters in Christ who are indwelt by the Spirit of God should experience unity based on the union they have with the triune God. John's hypothetical example in 4:20 is all too often very real. John calls the believer who claims to love God yet at the same time hates another believer "a liar." Such a one is not telling the truth. The reason for John's bold assertion is: "For the one who does not love his brother whom he has seen, cannot love God whom he has not seen" (v. 20).

A commandment from God follows: "The one who loves God should love his brother also" (4:21). The requirement for God's people to love one another whether they agree with them or not is not just a spiritual necessity; it is a command from God. Jesus gave a very similar command to His disciples (cf. John 13:34; 15:12). It is not only inconsistent behavior to say we love God and not love other members of the family of God, but it is flagrant disobedience of God's command.

Study Questions

1. Verse 12 tells us that "no one has beheld God at any time." If this is true, then who was appearing to men such as Abraham and Moses in the Old Testament?

2. How does John use the word *confesses* in verse 15?

3. When John says that our love is "perfected," what does he mean?

4. Which "day of judgment" is being spoken of in verse 17?

5. Give an example of a time when fear punished your heart.

6. What is the basis for unity in verse 20?

CHAPTER 11

Believers as Overcomers
1 John 5:1-8

Preview:
Wanting to win is very natural. Nobody wants to lose or be on a losing team. Despite this natural tendency, Satan often succeeds in creating a do-not-care atti- tude in Christians. He does this by killing the spirit, keeping us discouraged and defeated. In this section John teaches his readers that they can be overcomers because they are on God's side through faith in Jesus Christ. God's people need to remember that victory is in Him. John presents the basis, evidences, and results of the new birth as convincing reasons why believers are overcomers.

Basis and Evidence of the New Birth (5:1-3)

The chapter division seems a bit unnatural here. The discussion begun in 1 John 4 continues—one cannot say truthfully that he loves God unless he loves his brother and sister in the faith. John has already said that certain things will be true of a person who truly loves God (see discussion above of 4:11–19 and 4:20–21). Additional reasons for believers to show forth God's love are given in 5:1-8.

"Whoever believes that Jesus is the Christ is born of God; and whoever loves the Father loves the child born of Him" (5:1). Believing that Jesus is the Christ involves no work, for faith is not work. Yet the word *believes* here is not merely an intellectual acceptance of historic facts. These facts do not save; only Christ saves from sin. The belief referred to in 5:1 is personal and particular. It involves the recognition of oneself as totally lost and without merit before God and embracing Christ alone as Savior from sin. The belief that results in regeneration "not only admits an intellectual truth but enters into a direct relation with the powers of a spiritual order."[1]

The primary reason God's children are to love each other is because all who are His children have the same heavenly Father. The basis for loving each other is not because of agreements or even lifestyle. We are to love each other because we have the same heavenly Father. Love for others in the family of God is an evidence of the new birth.

Obedience to God's commandments is another evidence of the new birth. The present tense used in 5:2 emphasizes the continuous nature of loving God and keeping his commandments. The test of the genuineness and sincerity of our love is demonstrated by our obedience to God's Word. "Commandments" does not refer simply to the Ten Commandments. The word is used here as a broad reference to the Word of God (cf. John 15:10).

Keeping God's commandments, obeying God's Word, is a part of our love for God. "This is the love of God, that we keep His commandments" (1 John 5:3). Obedience, in other words, is a necessary and vital outcome of true love for God. Obedience always follows when the heart is really devoted to God. The kind of obedience spoken of here is not slavish, unwilling obedience. Rather, it is obedience that stems from a willing heart that longs to please God.

God's commandments are not "burdensome" (5:3). They can be obeyed. Though the child of God will sometimes find it difficult and often impossible to obey the commands of God, the Holy Spirit provides all that is needed to do all that God calls one to do.

Results of the New Birth (5:4–8)

The little children to whom John wrote were already overcomers. "For whatever is born of God overcomes the world; and this is the victory that has overcome the world—our faith" (5:4). The "world" refers to Satan's anti-God system in which all humans live. Victory over this *cosmos* comes from God to the believer through faith. Here then is another reason God's commandments are not burdensome.

The first use of the verb *overcomes* (v. 4) speaks of a continuous victory in a continuous struggle. The second use of the same word points to an individual specific temptation and victory. This is a play on words in the Greek text that is hard to reproduce in English.

One would expect John's "whatever" (5:4) to be "whoever." "This suggests that there is something inherently world-conquering in the very experience of being *born of God*. We are now immediately told what that is: 'And this is the victory that has overcome the world—our faith.'"[2]

The victory achieved at the time of faith in Christ as Savior is over Satan's "domain of darkness" and being transferred into the "kingdom of His beloved Son" (Col. 1:13). This describes a timeless condition. The fact that this is to be understood as taking place at the time of faith is substantiated by the use of the past tense of the last phrase of 1 John 5:4, "has overcome the world—our faith."

Jesus the Son of God (5:5) is Jesus the Christ (v. 1). A further description of Him and His work is given in verses 6 through 8. This Jesus the Christ who is the basis of the new birth "came by water and blood" (v. 6). There is general consensus among evangelicals that "by water" refers to His baptism and "by blood" refers to His death on the cross.

John the Baptist's baptism was unto repentance, but Christ had no sin of which to repent. Therefore, Christ's baptism was altogether unique. By submitting Himself to John and allowing him to baptize Him, Jesus was identifying Himself with John, His forerunner, and with his message of repentance. By so doing, Jesus was saying to Israel, "I agree with John: you need to repent and identify yourself with Me, the Messiah, for the kingdom of heaven is at hand."

The "kingdom of heaven" that John the Baptist, Jesus, the Twelve, and the Seventy proclaimed was the offer of the Davidic, earthly, messianic kingdom promised in 2 Samuel 7. The offer was a bona fide one and a contingent one. The contingency was that the national leaders must repent—that is, change their mind about themselves, their need, and who the Messiah was. They refused to repent, and therefore the kingdom was not established but will be established at the second coming of Christ to the earth (Rev. 19—20).

Also, at the time of His baptism, John the Baptist introduced Jesus to His public ministry. There was a public display of the empowering and anointing ministry of the Holy Spirit on Him. In 1 John the apostle was reminding his readers of historical facts that did not support the false view of Jesus that was preached by the false teachers of their day. The third witness of the incarnation of Christ the Son of God is the Holy Spirit (5:6). He is the truth just as Christ Himself is the truth (John 14:6).

John writes, "There are three that bear witness" (1 John 5:8). These three are the same as he has mentioned earlier—"the Spirit and the water and the blood" (v. 6). With special reference to the false teaching, which the little children were hearing, this threefold attestation of Jesus Christ verified that He was the incarnate Son of God. John flatly contradicts here the false teaching that Jesus was not God and not the Messiah and that therefore at the cross only the seemingly human Jesus died, not the Christ of God.

Study Questions

1. What is one of the tests or proofs that one is born of God?

2. How then are we to express our love for God?

3. In what way does John speak of the overcomer in verse 4?

4. At what time, in the life of the believer, does he or she gain the "victory that has overcome the world" (5:4)?

5. Which attribute of the Holy Spirit is stated in this section?

6. What is John referring to when he writes of the witness of "the Spirit and the water and the blood" (5:8)?

CHAPTER 12

The Father's Testimony of the Son
1 John 5:9-15

Preview:

Perhaps the greatest witness of the divinity of Christ is the testimony of His Father to that fact. Those who are saved know this witness to be true, while those who are unsaved deny this fact, effectively calling God a liar. This knowledge also confirms to the believer eternal life and the assurance that anything asked according to God's will shall be accomplished.

The Reality of the Testimony (5:9-10)

God the Father has given abundant testimony or witness of the identity of Jesus Christ—"the Spirit and the water and the blood" (5:8). John adds here another testimony of Him. He personally "has borne witness concerning His Son" (v. 9). This testimony is described in verses 11 and 12.

The "if" clause in verse 9 is not really raising a doubt. It does not introduce uncertainty concerning one's reception of the witness of other humans. The conditional Greek particle used here with the indicative mood assumes what is stated to be a fact. It could be translated "since."

"Receive" (5:9) means to accept in the sense of appropriate because we believe the testimony in question can be believed as truth. God's testimony is greater than any human's because it comes from Him. We should never hesitate to accept God's testimony. The striking contrast between accepting and not accepting God's testimony is set forth next (5:10). No doubt the testimony John is describing refers back to the testimony of the Spirit, the water, and the blood. Its primary reference, however, looks ahead to verses 11 and 12, where it is described in detail.

Those who receive the witness of God, yet to be disclosed, are those who believe on the Son of God. Those who do not believe make God out to be a liar (v. 10). When the witness or testimony of God is received, the receivers not only have the external witness in the Word but also the internal testimony of the Spirit in themselves (cf. Rom. 5:16; Gal. 4:6).

The Testimony Given (5:11–12)

The testimony God has given of His Son (5:9) is now stated in these verses. It consists of the spoken words of Christ to His own. Two grand and glorious statements of fact make up the testimony of God that is to be added to the testimony of the Spirit, the water, and the blood.

Writing to children of God, John says in verse 11 what was true of them. He was not offering them the gospel to be received. They had already received Christ by faith. The little children needed to be reminded that they had eternal life in Christ Jesus. Contrary to pre-Gnostic thinking, eternal life is not achieved by superior knowledge but in God's Son alone (John 3:36).

The first part of 1 John 5:12 is a further explanation of the last part of verse 11. The Greek definite article appears before the word *life* referring to a particular kind of life. God is the source of this eternal life, and only Jesus the Son of God can give it to believing sinners. In the Greek text, the words "the life" come before the verb. This makes them emphatic and stresses that no matter what other things a person may possess or be able to attain, he or she cannot acquire eternal life apart from Jesus Christ the Son of God. Spiritual life is in view in verses 11 and 12. Death does not mean cessation of life but separation of the material from the immaterial parts of man. Those who do not have the Son (v. 12) go on living eternally in the lake of fire prepared for the devil and his angels (Matt. 25:41, 46).

The Results of Receiving the Testimony (5:13–15)

Most likely "these things" in 1 John 5:13 refers primarily to the immediate context of verses 1–12. The same expression introducing why John has written specific things in this epistle occurs several times (cf. 1:4; 2:1, 26). Some understand the phrase in 5:13 to refer to everything written in the epistle to that point. It is significant that it is so near the end of the book and that no other occurrence of it follows. Also, John concluded his gospel in a similar way, summarizing the entire book (cf. John 20:31). There can be no question that John viewed the readers of his first epistle as those "who believe in the name of the Son of God" (5:13). They had been shaken and bombarded, however, by the revisionists and antichrists who said that Jesus was not the Christ and that they could not have eternal life. He writes to assure them that Jesus is the Christ and that they received eternal life when they trusted Him as Savior.

Stephen Smalley presents a balanced view of the meaning of "these things" (5:13): "This [verse] is transitional, in that it looks back to the subject matter of [verses] 5–12, and also provides a summary conclusion (to 1 John in its entirety) which leads into the closing remarks of [verses] 14–21."[1]

When the testimony of God is accepted, certain things follow. Trusting in what God says is true brings confidence (5:14). This is the fourth time in this epistle that John uses the term (cf. 2:28; 3:21; 4:17). The Greek term *parrēsia*, from which it comes means "boldness, courage, assurance." God is the One in whom John and the little children would have confidence.

Two specific aspects or results of this confidence in God follow. First, "If we ask anything according to His will, He hears us" (5:14). God's will sets boundaries to this promise. In some cases we can know God's will because of what God has said in His Word. But at other times we cannot determine God's will. James reminded his readers of their need to always preface their plans by considering God's will (James 4:13–17). God hears every prayer of His children prayed according to His will. Of that we can be certain.

The condition—praying according to God's will—is followed by a great promise: "And if we know that He hears us in whatever we ask, we know that we have the requests which we have asked from Him" (5:15). "We have the requests which we have asked from Him" must be understood in light of "according to His will" (v. 14). Jesus taught the same truth when He said, "Whatever you ask in My name, that will I do" (John 14:13).

Study Questions

1. Cite some Scripture verses in which God "has borne witness concerning His Son."

2. What are the implications of making God a liar?

3. Some sects within Christendom teach that the work of Jesus only starts the salvation process for believers, who must then perform works to complete the process. What does this section of 1 John teach in regard to this?

4. How does a believer in Christ gain the confidence John writes about in verse 14?

5. On what basis are requests granted (cf. John 14:13)?

6. What are the key concepts (or concept) that make it possible to have requests granted that are placed before God?

CHAPTER 13

A Call to Action
1 John 5:16-20

Preview:
The First Epistle of John ends as it began and continues throughout—a presen-
tation of truth and a call to live accordingly. John's call to action revolves around
two major areas—prayer and certainties in Christ.

Counsel Concerning Prayer (5:16-17)

John introduced the subject of prayer earlier in the chapter as one of the benefits of receiving the witness God gave of His Son (5:14-15). Before that, he
raised the prayer issue in 3:21-22. In the immediate context of this section,
5:14-15, John established the fact that the believer may have confidence in
prayer. Now in verses 16 and 17 he gives more specifics concerning prayer,
which is the believer's responsibility and privilege of communication with God.

Evangelical scholarship is divided over the interpretation of 5:16-17: "If
anyone sees his brother committing a sin not *leading* to death, he shall ask and
God will for him give life to those who commit sin not *leading* to death. There
is a sin *leading* to death; I do not say that he should make request for this."
One difficulty is what John means by "sin leading to death." First, it should
be noted that the Greek has no indefinite article *a*. Therefore, it should read
simply "sin," not "a sin" (vv. 16-17). Another problem is whether the death
John mentions is physical or spiritual. Also, is the *brother* in the passage referring to one's physical or spiritual brother?

Since the warning in 5:16–17 is given to believers, the promise that God will give life to those committing sin not leading to death does not refer to spiritual life, since they already had that. It would seem rather to refer to physical life. "Brother" in the passage speaks of another believer, not one's biological sibling, unless of course such a one is also a believer. Throughout the epistle *brother* and similar titles always refer to fellow believers.

The promise in verse 16 is that in answer to believing prayer God will not bring premature death to the believer who has committed sin not leading to death. John's whole purpose in 5:16–17 seems to be to urge his readers in intercessory prayer for one another. John is not exhorting believers to stop praying for those committing sin unto death. Believers ought to pray for any issue with confidence.

Verse 17 should be studied along with 3:4, which also presents a description of sin. In 5:17 it is "all unrighteousness is sin." In 3:4 it is "sin is lawlessness." Putting these two together, sin is not only opposition to God Himself; it is also opposition to His law, which reflects His character.

There is no indication given as to how exactly one is to determine which sins lead to death and which do not. We must appeal to other Scripture passages that teach that the Spirit of God prompts believers to pray. There are times when this ministry of the Spirit is absent. That may be an indication for that person not to pray.

Confession of Certainties (5:18–20)

While there may be some doubt as to when sin leads to physical death and when it does not, there are three absolute certainties for the believer in these verses. There are three *we know's* in verses 18 through 20.

Verse 18 is a restatement of the same truth in 3:9. "Know" speaks of certain and absolute knowledge. To be "born of God" describes believers. John has used this same and similar terminology several times in this epistle. The impartation and reception of divine life are in view.

There is widespread agreement that the phrase "No one who is born of God sins," refers to all believers. How to understand this is difficult, especially since John has just finished saying that brothers or believers can sin resulting in physical death (5:16). He also urged his readers to keep God's commandments so they would not sin (5:3–4). Earlier he told them to love one another so they would not sin (4:11–12), to abide in God by keeping His commandments (3:23–24), to walk in light rather than darkness (2:10–11), and to confess sin when it is committed (1:9).

Some resolve the problem by distinguishing between "who is born of God" (5:18) and "who was born of God" (5:18). Stephen Smalley is representative of this approach, making the latter phrase above refer to Christ.

Most commentators, however, assume (rightly, in our view) that by "the one who derives from God" John means Jesus Christ. . . . In favor of this view are the following points: (a) There is a logical change in tense from *ho gegennēmenos* (perfect; "anyone who has been born," describing the generation of a child of God) to *ho gennētheis* (aorist; literally, "the one who was born," referring to the specific event, in the past, of the birth of Jesus). (b) By using the same verb (*gennaō*, "to be born") to refer to Christ and the Christian, John may have wished to emphasize the identity of God's Son with his disciples (cf. 4:17); whereas the variation of tense mentioned in (a) marks an ultimate difference in the two sonships (cf. John 5:26; so Westcott, 194; see also Haas, Handbook, 128). This removes the objection that the singular expression *ho gennētheis* cannot apply to Jesus. (c) On the assumption that *ho gennētheis* refers to Jesus, the pronouns *auton* and *autou* allude to the protected believer in both cases; whereas, on the alternative view, a reflexive needs to be introduced in place of *auton* (as in some MSS; see the textual note above). (d) The concept of disciples being "protected," or "kept," by Jesus is found elsewhere in the NT (John 17:12; note also vv. 11, 15; Rev 3:10; cf. 1 Pet 1:5; Jude 24).[1]

Others resolve the difficulty by placing emphasis on the use of the present tense in the passage.

The perfect participle indicates that the new birth, far from being a transient phase of religious experience, has an abiding result. He who has been begotten of God remains God's child with permanent privileges and obligations. One of the obligations is expressed in the phrase that he *sinneth not*. The previous two verses (16, 17) concerning the sin unto death applied to unbelievers. Very different is the case of him who has been born of God. As in 3:4–10 . . . the tense of the verb is present and "implies continuity, habit, permanence" (Blaiklock). It expresses the truth, not that he cannot ever slip into acts of sin, but rather that he does not persist in it habitually or "live in sin" (Dodd). The new birth results in new behaviour. Sin and the child of God are incompatible. They may occasionally meet; they cannot live together in harmony.[2]

Zane Hodges views the above solution as an "example of overrefinement in the interpretation of the Greek tenses."[3] He offers in its place this answer to the problem:

It is reassuring to remember that, whatever our failures may be, they do not really touch what we are at the core of our being as God's children. In the last analysis our failures are due to the sinful "programming" of our earthly bodies, as Paul himself taught in Romans 7:7–25. Christians need to know this. At the very moment that we are most humbled by our sinful failures, and when we confess them, it is helpful to be confident that those failures have not really changed what we are as children of God.[4]

The reason given by John for his strong assertion in the first part of 5:18 is stated in the remainder of the verse: "He who was born of God keeps him." Because of that security "the evil one does not touch him." "Touch" (v. 18) is the translation of a strong word indicating to "lay hold of" (cf. John 20:17 where the same verb is used).

The second thing John and his readers were assured of expressed by "we know" was the awesome power of the evil one (5:19). Quite literally, the last part of the verse reads, "The whole world lies in the lap of the evil one." This wicked or *evil* one refers back to the evil one of verse 18. The entire world, John affirmed, is under satanic influence (cf. John 14:30). The description of the evil one is in direct contrast to the believer who is described as "of God."

As he concludes his first epistle, John appeals to the basic truth with which he began—the reality of the incarnation of the eternal Son of God. This is the third *we know* in John's conclusion. The false teachers were spreading their denials of the genuine humanity and absolute deity of the Lord Jesus Christ. John wrote to affirm what they already believed—"The Son of God has come" (1 John 5:20)—but they were being told it was not the truth. The emphasis is on the personal presence of Christ with the believers even though He had ascended and returned to the Father. Glenn Barker writes: "False teaching is ultimately 'apostasy from the true faith.' To follow after it is to become nothing better than an idol worshiper, especially if it is a matter of the truth of one's conception of God. The author is blunt. The false teachers propose not the worship of the true God, made known in his Son Jesus, but a false god—an idol they have invented."[5]

Through the work of the Holy Spirit—not mentioned here—the believer has been brought to know Christ. Through Him there has come an "understanding, in order that we might know Him who is true" (v. 20). Further, the believer has a personal relationship with Christ because he or she is "in Him who is true." About verse 20, John Gill writes:

> Christ is the true God, with his Father and the Spirit, in-distinction from all false, fictitious, or nominal deities; and such as are only by office, or in an improper and figurative sense; Christ is truly and really God, as

appears from all the perfections of Deity, the fullness of the Godhead being in him; from the divine works of creation and providence being ascribed to him.[6]

Study Questions

1. What are the two views as to how verses 16–17 are to be interpreted?

2. Which interpretation seems to make more sense to you? Why?

3. Does verse 18 teach that once you are born again you never sin again?

4. How extensive is the power of the evil one?

5. Why is John so adamant about his audience understanding that Jesus Christ, the Son of God, had come? What were they hearing?

CHAPTER 14

A Challenge to the Children of God
1 John 5:21

Preview:
John closes this epistle with a warm salutation by referring again to his readers as "little children." Throughout this letter, the apostle shows the utmost love and care for those he addresses. Here, he warns them to stay away from idols. He urges them to watch for themselves lest they be tempted to turn from the Lord and worship again false gods.

The same tender title given to John's readers in the beginning of the epistle (2:1) is given as he concludes (v. 21). The believers were *little born ones* because they were "born of God" (v. 18). In keeping with his warnings of things false, John concludes with an exhortation to "guard yourselves" (v. 21).

An idol, for a believer, is anything that comes between him or her and God. It is a substitute for God in the sense that it robs Him of first place.

Like so many apostolic exhortations, this, too, has the effective aorist imperative: "guard yourselves," let there be no question about it. The readers are to stand like armed guards ready to conquer every attack (2:13, 14; 4:4; 5:4, 5).[1]

This verse also refers to "the delusive and vain idols of the Cerinthian Gnosticism, whether ancient or modern; but it includes also the idols and false mediators of superstition, to whom the confidence is transferred which is due only to God in Christ."[2]

Though Henry Alford does not hold that a believer can lose his salvation, in strong language he writes this final warning and conclusion: "God's children are thus then finally warned of the consequence of letting go the only true God, in whom they can only abide by abiding in His Son Jesus Christ, in these solemn terms—to leave on their minds a wholesome terror of any the least deviation from the truth of God, seeing into what relapse it would plunge them."[3]

The early church was surrounded by raw paganism. Though one may be born again by God's Spirit, satanic temptation to go back and worship again false gods was strong. Since John had lived for so many years, he had witnessed all kinds of problems in the various assemblies scattered throughout Asia Minor. He probably knew well the struggles in the congregations in Italy, and in Palestine. Since he was the surviving apostle, many pilgrimages of pastors came to him for advice. In his final years as the pastor of the assembly at Ephesus, church history records that he was speechless, communicated by gesture, but also had to be carried about in a chair wherever he went.

When John died (circa A.D. 95), the Christian church went further into horrible persecution, both by the pagan citizens, and by the government authorities. The Roman emperors that followed in succession carried on the persecution began by Nero. Martyrdom was the order of the day. However, this did not stop the spread of Christianity. By the time of Constantine (325 AD), the church was well established throughout North Africa, parts of Asia, and in the far reaches of the Roman Empire. This small epistle would be important to help the churches remain faithful in living out the Christian life while suffering and laboring under burdensome circumstances.

As John completes this letter, his affection for the readers is obvious. His words served to remind his them of his heartfelt concerns, and of his abiding commitment to their welfare and spiritual growth. With his reminder to avoid idols, there is an overall warning against specific temptations, but also against heresy in general. "False teaching is ultimately 'apostasy from the true faith.' To follow after it is to become nothing better than an idol worshiper, especially if it is a matter of the truth of one's conception of God. The author is blunt. The false teachers propose not the worship of the true God, made known in his Son Jesus, but a false god—an idol they have invented."[4] False teaching appears to have been a prominent weakness in the early congregations. The churches had not been firmly established and grounded. With warm words, but also with great personal concern, John closes this important epistle that would shore up the direction of the fledgling congregations.

Study Questions

1. Why does John exhort the believers to guard themselves?

2. In what way is this epistle particularly directed at fledgling congregations?

SECTION 2

Love in Action

The Book of Second John

CHAPTER 15

Background of Second John

Author

The human penman introduces himself as "the elder" (2 John 1:1). There is overwhelming agreement among ancient writers that "the elder" refers to the apostle John. Zane Hodges' summary of higher critical opposition to this opinion is helpful.

> The efforts made by critical scholarship to find non-apostolic authors for the Fourth Gospel and the epistles are perhaps not surprising, due to scholarship's usual bias against apostolic eyewitness accounts. But the attempt to differentiate the authorship of the Gospel from that of the epistles and even, sometimes, that of First John from Second and Third John, is a stunning display of tunnel vision. It would be hard to find four books anywhere in Greek literature that exhibit a style more likely to stem from one mind than does the style of the Gospel and the epistles. Even the English reader can detect this, but in Greek the impression of a single writer is overwhelming. This being the case, the strong support given by ancient tradition to authorship by John the son of Zebedee for both the Gospel and the epistles should be seen, not as two sets of evidence but as a single voice.[1]

There is considerable evidence that John the apostle was in Ephesus during the last years of his life. Many therefore believe that all three of his epistles were written from Ephesus about the same time.[2]

Date

It is generally agreed that the three epistles were all written about the same time, around A.D. 90. Hodges places the possible date for the writing of the epistles considerably earlier— A.D. 64 to 65.[3]

Recipients

The letter was addressed to "the chosen lady and her children" (v. 1). Two
basic views are held in regard to the meaning of this phrase. Some believe
"chosen lady" refers to a local church, possibly the church at Ephesus. The
"chosen sister" (v. 13) would then refer to another local church. Others
believe John was addressing an individual believer and her biological family.
This view seems most popular.

> In all likelihood both letters were sent to churches under John's pastoral
> care in the province of Asia. There is nothing to compel the conclusion
> that they were directed to the same congregation. The identity of the "elect
> lady" is debatable. Some have preferred to make "lady" a proper name,
> Kuria. Others have favored the view that "elect lady" is not a reference to
> an individual but to a church (cf. 1 Pet. *5:13),* and are able to point to
> such things as the use of the plural in verses 8, 10, and 12 (although the
> singular is used in v. 5) and the fact that the lady and her children are
> known and loved by all who know the truth (v. 1). On the other hand,
> the allusion to the sister of the addressee (v. 13) seems to favor an indi-
> vidual, and if she were a very prominent person it is not unthinkable that
> the church throughout the region (v. 1) would be acquainted with her
> and her family. A decision is not easy here, and the matter should proba-
> bly be left open.[4]

It seems better to hold that John was writing to a particular assembly of
believers and not one person in a local church.[5]

Theme

This letter is straightforward and to the point. It is an admonition to hold on
to and retain what they had received earlier. There is also the repeated warning against those promoting deception, those who had left various congregations and returned to the world. Some of these people were actually missionaries of evil. Some men are not to be received by the churches, in fact, they are
not even to be greeted or welcomed in the assemblies, or in the homes of the
people. The false teachers are the same John wrote about in his first letter.
Gnosticism was a growing concern. It was a heresy of the first order. It was a
mysterious belief that could be found in various forms in other religions. It
often took on the patterns of Christianity and was devastating to sound doctrine. Gnostics were said to be followers of Cerinthus and denied the deity of
Christ. It appears that Diotrephes (3 John 1:9) leaned toward the Gnostics
and wanted their missionaries sheltered and aided rather than the workers

sent out from John. There is still a question as to how deep into Gnosticism Diotrephes had ventured. Though he may not have accomplished his desire to come to those he was writing to, John wrote that he wanted to settle some of this confusion when he arrived (2 John 1:14).

This is a precious and important epistle because it puts flesh and blood into the mix of doctrinal problems. Also, this letter along with all of the New Testament letters, have the stamp of the inspiration of the Holy Spirit on them. Though short, they are a vital part of the Word of God and they give important glimpses of what the churches were facing. All three of John's epistles show in an obvious way his concerns about what the detractors are doing to try to destroy the faith. Some have observed that even in John's Gospel, there are hints that he was addressing the coming destruction of Gnosticism. Here in his epistles, this same war is raging!

In these letters of 2 and 3 John, "we catch a glimpse of John's activity in his old age. They present a little piece of church history. John has an unpleasant task and he performs it. Missionaries are still pressing forward farther and farther. Third John 5-8 is a rich missionary text; and verses 9-12 ought to interest every church official."[6]

Both 2 John and 3 John have themes of love and truth. Second John, however, seems to emphasize Christian love with its foundation in truth. This short letter deals with three aspects of Christian love, which is based in truth: responsive love, obedient love, and discerning love.

Outline of Second John

I. Responsive Love (2 John 1:1–3)

II. Obedient Love (2 John 1:4–6)

III. Discerning Love (2 John 1:7–11)

IV. Conclusion (2 John 1:12–13)

CHAPTER 16

Responsive Love
2 John 1:1-3

Preview:

For John to write of God's love is second nature. He begins this letter with a greeting that marries love with truth (a biblical pairing emphasized by John).

In this short letter, the apostle raises many important practical and spiritual issues. First, there is the warm greeting to a prominent Christian woman and her family. She and her family had been active in setting for and advocating what was true about the faith (vv. 1-3). John has a warm attachment to them, and as well, he expresses joy and gratitude not only because they have so responded to the truth, but also because they were walking in it with faithful integrity (v. 4). John then urges his readers to life in warm, mutual love, and in obedience to the great commandment of Christ (vv. 5-6). John then refers to so many deceivers who had gone into the world. He warns against the subtleties of their deception (vv. 7-8). The apostle then gives a test as to their true character (v. 9), and then adds that they are not to be given any form of hospitality, or any friendliness toward their teachings (vv. 10-11). He then closes with a statement that he hoped to come to the elect lady soon and that he would not write any more to her (vv. 12-13).

John did not use his personal name in his greeting. Instead, he used "the elder" (v. 1), which is more of a title. It described both his age and his official position. His first readers, apparently, knew him by this title.

John is "the Presbyter" because the churches gave him this title in an eminent sense as we speak of "the President," "the Governor," etc. When they titled John in this manner the churches intended to *honor* the *aged* apostle who *alone* had survived the other apostles. This honor was combined with the recognition of John's apostolic authority as being that of the one apostle who still remained to guide, teach, and direct the churches. Because he understood it in this sense, John accepted the title. When one said "the Presbyter," all the members of the churches knew who was meant; when here and in Third John, John himself writes "the Presbyter," the readers know who this is. The addition "John" is not only unnecessary but would also be misleading, for it would convey the thought that there were others like him, save that they had other names such as "the Presbyter this," "the Presbyter that" but all were equally eminent men. This was not true; there was only this one "the Presbyter," and there were no others who were to be ranked with him.[1]

The letter is addressed to "the chosen lady" (v. 1). Some students of the epistle believe this was a reference to an individual person. Others think the phrase describes a particular local assembly, a personification of a church. The latter view seems more likely. John must have had some special responsibility over the believers in that assembly. "John's language is not appropriate to a real person, either in his statement of love (1, 2) or in his exhortation to love (5). The elder could hardly refer to his personal love for a lady and her children as a 'commandment . . . which we had from the beginning' (see 5)."[2]

In this church view the "chosen sister" (v. 13) would refer to another local church. If the letter had been addressed to a woman in the church, the "sister" would then point to that woman's physical sister.

The Old Testament uses similar language to refer to Israel (Lam. 1:6, 15; 2:11, 13). In the New Testament the universal church or body of Christ is called the "bride" of Christ (Rev. 19:7–8; 22:17). Even the Corinthian assembly was described as a "chaste virgin" (2 Cor. 11:2).

John loved this local church, and called its members "her children" (2 John 1:1). The pronoun *I* is in the emphatic position. In this way, John may have been setting himself apart from the heretics who were peddling their false doctrines to these people. John truly, loved these people. It was God's truth that bound John to this house church, especially the truth about the person and work of Christ (cf. 1 John 2:21–23). John loved all who embraced the truth. On this woman and her children, Barnes writes: "All those Christians who had an opportunity of knowing them were sincerely attached to them. It would seem, from a subsequent part of the epistle, (v. 10) that this female was of a hospitable character, and was accustomed to entertain at her house the professed friends of [Christianity], especially [the] religious teachers, and it is probably that she was the more extensively known from this fact."[3]

Next, John gives a reason why those who knew the truth loved the members of this church. It was "for the sake of the truth which abides in us and will be with us forever" (v. 2). This is in contrast to things that pass away. This stated reason shows that biblical love is vitally associated with revealed truth. God's truth is at home in the believer and remains so forever.

A strong affirmation follows in verse 3: "Grace, mercy and peace will be with us, from God the Father and from Jesus Christ, the Son of the Father, in truth and love." *Grace* is God's unmerited favor. *Mercy* is God's withholding deserved punishment. *Peace* is the restoration of harmony with God that accompanies salvation. Kistemaker observes: "Paul uses similar greetings (with only slight variations) in his letters to Timothy. However, John is more articulate when he places Jesus Christ on the same level as God the Father. John repeats the word *from* and notes that Jesus is the Son of God the Father."[4]

God the Father and Jesus Christ both bestow on the redeemed ones grace, mercy, and peace. Jesus Christ is "the Son of the Father" (v. 3). This is a unique expression used here, no doubt, to alert the readers of the teaching of those John calls "deceivers" (v. 7) who do "not have God" (v. 9). In this way John reminds the readers of the full and absolute deity of the Lord Jesus Christ.

Truth makes love discriminating. Love must not cause us to betray or undermine truth or even to neglect it. Neither of these essentials must be pursued at the expense of the other.

Responsive love, a fruit of the Spirit, is also to be obedient love. On this verse Kistemaker concludes: "John's greeting deviates considerably from that of the rest of the writers of the New Testament epistles. Paul, Peter, and Jude convey their greeting in the form of a prayer or a wish: "Grace and peace be yours in abundance" (e.g., 1 Peter 1:2; 2 Peter 1:2). But John is definite, because he does not express a wish but declares that "grace, mercy and peace . . . will be with us." He adds the words "in truth and love."[5]

Study Questions

1. What is the theme of 2 John?

2. Who is "the chosen lady" John addresses?

3. What does John mean when he says, "Truth abides in us . . . forever"?

4. What is this "truth" of which John speaks?

CHAPTER 17

Obedient Love
2 John 1:4-6

Preview:
John adds a third element to his formula of love and truth, obedience to God's commandments, identifying "loving one another" as a commandment.

John rejoiced for those in the assembly who were walking in truth. He found out about these who were faithful either by a personal visit or more likely from someone else who had visited them. "I was very glad to find *some* of your children walking in truth" (v. 4). "Very glad" could be translated "overjoyed." The word is found also in 3 John 3. "Some" needs to be supplied because of the construction here. The implication seems to be that some in the fellowship, no doubt those who held to deviant views of the person of Christ, were not walking or living according to truth. John, the elder, included himself with those who received the commandment from God to so live and obeyed it (cf. 1 John 2:7; 3:23; 4:7, 21; 5:2–3). "The presbyter ascribes the 'command' (to live in truth and love) to the Father, rather than directly to Jesus (cf. John 13:34; 15:12, 17), because he is the ultimate source of the message declared by Jesus (John 7:16–17) and his disciples (1 John 1:5)."[1]

That which John was asking this church for was not a new commandment. It was the "one which we have had from the beginning" (v. 5). The commandment John and his readers had from the beginning was to "love one another" in the family of God. To the commandment to believe in verse 4 is added the commandment to love (v. 5). These two, faith and love, are evidences of the new birth. "Christian faith is an obedient response to God's self-revelation in Christ. This revelation has a moral content. If men hate the light, it is because their deeds are evil (John 3:19–21). . . . Similarly, Christian love belongs rather to the sphere of action than of emotion. It is not an involuntary, uncontrollable passion, but unselfish service undertaken by deliberate choice."[2]

Love and Obedience in John's Writings	
God is love.	1 John 4:8
The Father loves the Son, for the Son keeps the Father's commands.	John 3:35; 5:20; 10:17
God loved us first.	1 John 4:19
God loved the world and gave His only-begotten Son.	John 3:16
The Father loves those who love and obey His Son.	John 14:24; 16:21
The one who loves Christ will keep His commandments.	John 14:21
The one who keeps Christ's commandments is the one who truly loves Him.	John 14:23; 2 John 1:6
The one who keeps Christ's commandments is the one who abides in His love.	John 15:10; 1 John 2:5
Christ's disciples are to love one another.	John 13:34, 35; 15:12, 17; 1 John 3:10, 11, 14, 16–18, 23; 4:7, 8, 11, 12, 20, 21; 5:1; 2 John 1:5
Christ's disciples truly love one another when they keep God's commandments.	1 John 5:2, 3
Those who love the world and the things of the world do not have the Father's love in them.	1 John 2:15

The description of the love John has in mind follows: "And this is love, that we walk according to His commandments" (v. 6). We can do nothing more or better for our Christian brothers and sisters than to live obedient to God. If we live according to God's commandments, we will love one another. It is as simple as that.

Obedience to God's commandments can be summarized in one commandment, to obey Him as He has told us to do in His Word, "just as you have heard from the beginning" (v. 6). There is no room here for any alteration or revision of God's commands. Zane Hodges suggests correctly that this may have been intended for the revisionists who would revise the command so as to justify any compromise with idolatry.[3]

In addition to responsive love and obedient love, John also wrote about discerning love.

> John defines "the love" that is referred to in this commandment which his readers had had ever since they became Christians; *ina* is again appositional. It is this, "that we walk according to his (the Father's) commandments." Loving one another is not one doing of one commandment among many others; it is doing all God's commandments. But we should not think of the Mosaic law but of the gospel and of what it asks of us. We are walking in the whole gospel when we love one another as brethren in Jesus Christ, God's Son. John writes, "that we walk" in the love that is hidden in the heart. This love displays itself in our walk in word and in deed. John repeats and thus emphasizes this word.[4]

It had been reported to the apostle that most of the congregation was walking in doctrinal truth. Because he speaks about the source of this truth, he does not need to repeat it in 3 John 1:3, 4. Because of Diotrephes and many others, and their flirting with Gnosticism, John shows his joy that they are walking in the truth. This heretical group with whom Diotrephes was relating to, did not even have the Father because they were denying the divine nature of the Son (1 John 2:23).

Study Questions

1. What are the two views of who these "children" are?

2. When did John learn this commandment spoken of in verse 5?

3. In verse 6, is John referring to the commandments given to Israel at Mount Sinai?

CHAPTER 18

Discerning Love
2 John 1:7–13

Preview:
John explains how deceivers, or false teachers, may be identified by their lack of obedience to God's commandments. He warns concerning Gnostics in particular and advises on proper godly behavior when confronted with their heresy.

Verse 7 begins with *for* (*hoti*). This is not meant as a connection with the verse just before. It is rather to be understood as being tied to the verse that follows, verse 8. John is in that verse giving a reason why a caution is given. It is truth that many deceivers had been exposed, and they are going to various places scattering error. Believers are to be aware and avoid doctrinal betrayal and ruin. Because there were so many false teachers and seditious missionaries abroad, the church had to be constantly on guard. Looking back on the history of the early church, it is rather startling as to how quickly heresy arose, but this would be a sign of things to come. The church would continue to wrestle with false teachings and departure from the truth.

Because "many deceivers have gone out into the world" (v. 7) John's readers have reason to heed the admonitions of verses 5 and 6. Christ Himself warned of false Christs and false prophets to come (Mark 13:22–23). Some of these had already come and were damaging the believers by revising God-given truths to suit their own views.

The deceivers did "not acknowledge Jesus Christ as coming in the flesh" (v. 7). John not only calls them deceivers but also "antichrist" (cf. 1 John 4:2–3). Although full-blown Gnosticism was not yet in existence, the seeds of insipid Gnosticism were present. Denial of the incarnation of the Son of God resulted in denial of both the humanity and deity of Christ.

R. C. H. Lenski comments:

> *Hoti* introduces an independent sentence just as *we*, too, use "because." It states the reason that John is writing all this. In 1 John 4:1 he says: "Many pseudo-prophets have gone out into the world"; here he calls them "deceivers" and uses the simple aorist. Not content to be deceived themselves, these men cannot rest until they have deceived others, as many as possible. They do not bother pagans; their prey are true Christians. "Into the world" means far and wide in the world, wherever they find Christians. They "went out" means from their leader Cerinthus, from his headquarters; some take it that they went out from the devil, the archdeceiver.[1]

The present participle used with the *coming* of Christ in the flesh seems to include His past coming, His present continuous resurrected ministry, and His future coming.

The presence of the deceivers prompted a warning from John: "Watch yourselves, that you might not lose what we have accomplished, but that you may receive a full reward" (v. 8). This introduces the warning to the faithful in view of the false teachers in their midst. John's readers needed to be vigilant, on their guard for false teaching. The same verb is used of Jesus' warning in Mark 13:22–23.

Because they were the messengers of the Lord Jesus, the apostles always felt responsible for the spiritual lives of the flocks (Phil. 2:6), even though not all of them planted churches. They also sent out missionaries who reported to them what was happening in the fledgling congregations. For example, the apostle Paul did not start all the Christian assemblies in Rome and Colosse. Yet, he was involved in what was taking place doctrinally as these churches grew and struggled.

Because John was in charge of the message that was "from the beginning," all his labors were then occupied with keeping the truth going forth of the Lord Jesus Christ having come in the flesh. It was incumbent upon John as an apostle to guard the truth. After all, he was one of the few who had witnessed the Lord transfigured in all His divine glory. In a real sense, then, it was appropriate that he was the last of the "witnessing" apostles and disciples of Jesus. Because of his status as an apostle, one can understand his great concern for the churches to be on guard against false teaching and error.

Simon Kistemaker writes:

> Already in his first epistle, John warns the readers to test the spirits: "Every spirit [teaching] that acknowledges that Jesus Christ has come in the flesh

is from God, but every spirit that does not acknowledge Jesus is not from God" (4:2–3). Even though there is similarity between this passage and that of 2 John 7, the difference in the verb forms *has come* (1 John 4:2) and *as coming* (2 John 7) is obvious. The one verb is in the past tense, the other in the present. Is there a difference in meaning? Hardly. The past tense describes Jesus' earthly ministry, and the present tense is a descriptive term about Christ. In the New Testament, the expression *the one who is coming* is a messianic designation (e.g., Matt. 11:2; John 1:15, 27; 12:13; Rev. 1:4). Thus, John applies the present tense of the participle *coming* to Jesus Christ as a testimony to anyone who denies this truth.[2]

There seems to be a definite connection between holding on to truth and receiving a full reward. John did not want his friends to lose the full reward from God for their work. John was not referring to losing eternal life. Rather, he was pointing to the *bema* or Judgment Seat of Christ (cf. Rom. 14:10; 1 Cor. 3:10–16; 2 Cor. 5:10). This judgment comes after the rapture of the church (1 Cor. 15:51–58; 1 Thess. 4:13–18) and takes place in heaven while the seventieth week of Daniel or the time of Jacob's trouble (Jer. 30:7) is being fulfilled on earth (cf. Rev. 6–16).

Most evangelical expositors of 2 John 1:9 believe John was warning that those who do not remain in the teaching of Christ are not believers. They may have professed to be believers, but they give evidence that they only had a profession and not a possession because they do not abide in Christ's teaching. This view is bolstered by John's statement that such do "not have God" (v. 9). On the contrary, those who abide in Christ's teaching have "both the Father and the Son." The false teachers about whom John writes here proposed that they had superior knowledge and had advanced into new regions of truth. They were suggesting that the believers leave the old teaching and replace it with the new.[3]

Zane Hodges, a Greek scholar, and some others hold an entirely different view. They hold that verse 9 and other verses, especially in 1 John, teach that those not remaining in the teaching of Christ are not lost if they have truly trusted Christ as Savior earlier. They do not believe faith in Christ has to be ongoing. A true believer may even later deny Christ's person and work.

Zane Hodges puts it this way: "The person who does not abide in the true doctrine about Jesus Christ does not have God with him in his new perspective and/or lifestyle. More bluntly, he is out of touch with God, while he who abides in the doctrine of Christ is vitally in touch with God, i.e., this person has both the Father and the Son."[4]

The warning of verse 11 is a serious one indeed. John does not seem to be warning against showing hospitality to those in need. Rather, he is referring to those who are making it their business to expose believers in house churches to their so-called advanced understanding of Christ. It appears that these deceivers and antichrists (v. 7) were professionals. The warning (v. 11) is that those who give such people their blessing and allow them a platform are guilty of participating in their evil deeds. In other words, the believers are to separate from false teachers, not cooperate with them. To bid false teachers Godspeed is to share in their work (cf. 3 John 1:8).

> This command has been by some laid to the fiery and zealous spirit of St. John, and it has been said that a true Christian spirit of love teaches us otherwise. But as rightly understood, we see that this is not so. Nor are we at liberty to set aside direct ethical injunctions of the Lord's Apostles in this manner. Varieties of individual character may play on the surface of their writings: but in these solemn commands which come up from the depths, we must recognize the power of that One Spirit of Truth which moved them all as one. It would have been infinitely better for the Church now, if this command had been observed in all ages by her faithful sons.[5]

Conclusion (2 John 1:12–13)

John assumed that given his readers' knowledge of him and his teaching he would be welcomed and received by them (v. 12). The contrast between how they were to respond to truth and truth-tellers and error and those who knowingly promote it is stark. John's presence in the assembly would result in abounding joy for them.

John passed on greetings from other house churches to his readers. If "chosen lady" (v. 1) refers to a specific local assembly of believers, then "children of your chosen sister" (v. 13) refers to members of another local assembly or assemblies.

Lenski offers this summary:

> **There salute thee the children of thy sister, the elect one,** all the members of the church in whose midst John is writing, which we take to be Ephesus. By calling this church "thy sister" John means *that* this church in Ephesus is also full mistress in her domain. Although as "the Elder" he resides in this congregation, and because of this fact, there is no boss there to lessen joy. By calling this Ephesian kuria "the elect one" (note the emphasis conveyed by the second article) John stresses the high position and the obligation that belong to both congregations, each is equally "a mistress elect" of the Lord.[6]

And Kistemaker also concludes:

The elder (John) sends greetings to a distinguished lady and her children. He expresses his joy about the obedience some of her children have shown in honoring the truth. He admonishes her to be steadfast in fulfilling the command to love one another and to obey God's precepts. He alerts her to the dangers that numerous deceivers pose to her, and encourages her to guard her spiritual possessions. He warns her not to have fellowship with these teachers who do not bring the teachings of Christ. If she welcomes them into her house, she promotes the cause of these false teachers. He concludes his letter with the remark that he hopes to visit her. He sends greetings from the children of the chosen sister of the lady he addresses.[7]

These final verses make up the close of this epistle with what would be a normal wish. John the elder indicates he has more to say, but he realizes that it would have a greater impact if he delivered his thoughts in person. The phrase "face to face," (actually *mouth to mouth*) implies an intimate and close sharing of both feelings and facts. But there is something more he wishes to add. In the Christian community there is the need for continuing and meaningful joy and fellowship in Christ. In the case of the final verse, a large family must have come to faith in Christ. John was relating to them. It is quite possible to imagine that many of the relatives associated in this clan had assisted John, given him financial help, and provided hospitality when he traveled, and certainly prayed for him and stayed in contact by letter. John may be dealing with several generations of believers who had passed their faith down from parent to child. The apostle may have watched these family members grow in wisdom and maturity. The elect lady and her larger family may have been perfect candidates for sharing the important messages and teachings of this letter with others. Christianity had quickly become a family matter!

Study Questions

1. More than likely, who are the deceivers John writes about?

2. Who or what is John referring to when he writes of "the antichrist"? See also 1 John 2:18.

3. What does verse 9 teach us about teachers that may be within the Church even today?

4. What is the "house" John is speaking of in verse 10?

5. What is a believer doing if he or she knowingly fellowships with a false teacher?

6. What overall spiritual impression do you have from reading and studying this short letter?

SECTION 3

Response to Truth

The Book of Third John

CHAPTER 19

Background of Third John

Similarities exist between 2 John and 3 John. The problem that prompted the writing of both seems to be how believers were to treat and respond to itinerant teachers. Therefore Christian truth and love are chief concerns in both letters. Each letter contains fewer than three hundred Greek words and was most likely written on a single sheet of papyrus.

Important differences can also be found in the two letters. As noted in the commentary on 2 John, the evidence seems to support that it was addressed to a local body of believers—a house church. Third John, on the other hand, is addressed to an individual and is more personal than 2 John. With the mention of three individuals—Gaius, Diotrephes, and Demetrius—we get a closer look at interpersonal relationships in the first-century church.

Three friends of Paul are named Gaius. There is the Gaius of the Corinthian church (1 Cor. 1:14), the Gaius of Macedonia (Acts 19:29), and the Gaius of Derbe (20:4). However, many commentators have speculated that this is not the Gaius mentioned by Paul. Though not a lot is known about the three personalities sketched out in this letter, they become interesting characters in light of how John deals with them. He mentions herein Gaius, Diotrephes, and Demetrius. Gaius is the reliable layperson, Diotrephes is the upfront church official, and Demetrius is seen as a kind and thoughtful messenger from Ephesus carrying a letter. John is the last apostle and disciple of Christ serving as the elder pastor in that city. He is shown here keeping a sharp eye out for the doctrinal direction of the churches. Here he is also greatly concerned with the Gnostic heretics and deceivers who are at work as he mentioned in the other two letters.

Date and Author

It is generally believed that John spent the last years of his life in Ephesus. After writing his gospel, he wrote 1, 2, and 3 John. Both 2 and 3 John were very likely written before the terrible persecution of Domitian's reign in A.D. 95. The date, therefore, seems to have been in the late 80s or early 90s. Some evangelicals assign an earlier date with substantial reasons. The exact date, therefore, as well as the place from which 1, 2, and 3 John were written, must be left as open questions.[1]

Purpose and Theme

John, under the Spirit's direction, sensed that Gaius needed encouragement to continue to extend hospitality to Demetrius. There apparently was some friction among believers over the issue of showing hospitality to traveling teachers. John's personal letter to Gaius provided instruction for settling the dispute.

As noted in the commentary on 2 John, love was the overriding theme in that letter. Here in 3 John truth seems to occupy the place of prominence. Truth is not absent in 2 John; neither is love absent in 3 John. Rather, John's emphasis differs in these two letters.

This short personal letter is easily divided into three responses to truth—by Gaius (vv. 1–8), by Diotrephes (vv. 9–11), and by Demetrius (v. 12)—with concluding remarks by John in verses 13 and 14.

> In 2 John the Elder writes to the elect lady and her children, commending her for the fidelity to the truth manifested in certain of her children, and reminding her of the commandment of love in which she and others are to walk. He seeks to impress upon her also the importance of holding the doctrine of Christ as the incarnate Son of God and of refusing fellowship and aid to those who do not hold this doctrine and yet pose as Christian teachers.
>
> Third John, addressed to a man named Gaius, praises him for his stand on behalf of the truth and for his kindness to traveling brethren who are active in the service of the Lord. Gaius is in pleasing contrast to a certain Diotrephes, who possibly belongs to the same local church. This man has refused to show hospitality to the workers sent forth with the author's blessing. Indeed, he has arbitrarily excluded from the church those who have received such missionaries. He will hear from the author when the latter is able to come in person to the church and deal with the situation. The body of the letter concludes with a commendation of a certain Demetrius.[2]

Outline of Third John

I. The Response of Gaius to Truth (3 John 1:1-8)

II. The Response of Diotrephes to Truth (3 John 1:9-11)

III. The Response of Demetrius to Truth (3 John 1:12-14)

CHAPTER 20

The Response of Gaius to Truth
3 John 1:1-8

Preview:

The apostle John addresses a believer named Gaius, "whom I love in truth." That he and others are walking in truth seems to be very important to John. He also commends Gaius on his treatment of the brethren, especially evangelists who pass through on their mission.

As in his introduction and greeting in 2 John, so here the author calls himself "the elder" (v. 1). This was not John's personal name but rather the title by which he was known to his readers.

The order of the Greek words in verse 1 is "The elder to Gaius, the beloved." In four out of the fourteen verses in this letter John refers to Gaius in this way (vv. 1, 2, 5, and 11). This man was special and was loved dearly by John and his fellow saints. John loved Gaius "in truth." The basis of his love was not emotion but truth.

On verse 1 Kistemaker writes:

This is the address on the envelope, so to speak. The writer calls himself "the elder" (see also 2 John 1) and he sends his letter to his friend Gaius. The address, however, is very brief because the sender omits the names of places. That is, although we may assume that John resided in Ephesus, we have no knowledge of where Gaius lived. . . .

John writes that he loves Gaius in the truth (compare 2 John 1). The relationship between the elder and Gaius was one of love and trust. John twice mentions that he loves Gaius, for a literal translation of the text says,

"To Gaius the beloved, whom I love in truth." Gaius is loved by God and loved by John because of the truth which Gaius professes. This brief remark apparently takes the place of a greeting. In distinction from other personal letters, this epistle lacks the familiar salutation *grace, mercy and peace* or its equivalent. After the address, John expresses a wish.[1]

Several men in the New Testament are called Gaius. We read of Gaius of Corinth (1 Cor. 1:14), Gaius from Macedonia (Acts 19:29), and Gaius of Derbe (Acts 20:4). Some argue strongly that the Gaius in 3 John was the one from Derbe. We cannot be certain, however, that the Gaius of verse 1 can be identified with any with the same name in the New Testament.

On verse 1 R. C. H. Lenski summarizes:

"The Elder" and the relative clause "whom I on my part love in connection with truth" are the same as those found in 2 John 1, which see. Note that John loves whomever he loves only in connection with what is truth (*anarthrous*). His love is governed by this truth even as his love is that of true comprehension and corresponding purpose. All that we know about the Gaius who is here addressed is contained in this letter. We can safely say that he is not one of those men of this name who are mentioned elsewhere in the New Testament.[2]

The phrase introduced by "beloved" in verse 2 was a common introduction in letters of that time.[3] In view of this, we need not think Gaius was ill when John wrote. Pagans who included this kind of note in their greeting prayed to their gods. John wished for Gaius that his physical condition would equal that of his soul's health. "Soul" (v. 2) refers to the seat of affections and impressions, the immaterial part. *Soul, spirit,* and *heart* are sometimes used interchangeably in the New Testament.

John was assured of Gaius' spiritual health because of good reports from "brethren" (v. 3) who came and gave testimony to John. These brethren very likely could have been some to whom Gaius had shown hospitality (vv. 5–8). This news brought rejoicing to John's heart, for the testimony he received was centered in the truth by which Gaius ordered his life.

It seems certain that Gaius was a convert of John. John expressed to Gaius that nothing brought more joy to him than to hear that his children walked in truth (v. 4). Thus, it seems that John the elder counted Gaius as one of his children in the faith. Some feel, however, that since John referred to his readers in 1 John as "my little children," he only meant to count Gaius as one of his spiritual children under his tutelage. Barnes concurs:

We may . . . infer that Gaius had been converted under the ministry of John, and that he was probably a much younger man than he was. John, the aged apostle, says that he had no higher happiness than to learn, respecting those who regarded him as their spiritual father, that they were steadfast in their adherence to the doctrines of [Christianity]. The same thing may be said now of all the ministers of the gospel, that their highest comfort is found in the fact that those to whom they minister, whether still under their care or removed from them, persevere in a steadfast attachment to the true doctrines of religion.[4]

From his general commendation of Gaius, John becomes specific. He does this by the mention of Gaius's faithfulness toward "the brethren and especially when they are strangers" (v. 5). Since these to whom Gaius showed hospitality gave testimony of the same before "the church" (v. 6), they undoubtedly were believers.

"The brethren" (v. 6) seems clearly to refer to traveling evangelists from the vicinity where Gaius lived. The "strangers" (v. 6), on the other hand, were not at all well known to Gaius and apparently not to John either. Without naming any in either of these categories, John was no doubt referring to a large number to whom Gaius showed Christian hospitality. "Obviously, Gaius was a host whose hospitality was warm and ungrudging, so that he conveyed a true spirit of Christian love to those whom he entertained and assisted. He was what Paul would call a *cheerful giver* (2 Cor. 9:7)."[5]

It seems as if Diotrephes did not like Gaius because of his putting up and assisting the missionaries of John in their travels. Since John is asking Gaius to continue this work, and to bring this letter with him on his way, Diotrephes will dislike Gaius even more. To have the trust of this great disciple of Christ, John, and to enjoy his trust, favor and love, must have been seen as a special blessing beyond measure. Meanwhile, it seems as if the love of Diotrephes is turning more to the Gnostic heresy and those propagating this error.

As far as their travel is concerned, it must be remembered that the missionaries traveled at their own expense, except when generosity is given them by other believers. When the entire church put forth contributions the burden was not carried by everyone in the membership. As this letter goes on, it will be shown that Diotrephes was trying to stop the assembly from doing its part. Thus, John prays that the Lord will continue to prosper Gaius so that he may continue to be helpful in the mission endeavor.

John desires health and prosperity for Gaius for spiritual reasons and not simply for the pampering of the flesh. In contrast, the state of Diotrephes' soul was in such a sad state that he had no love for John. Instead, he tried to subvert the missionary work of the apostle in acting as a tyrant against those he wanted to assist.

Gaius put his love for the Lord and His servants into practice. The believing travelers he had helped told the local church members about his generosity (v. 6). Earlier they testified of his living according to the truth of God (v. 3). John praised Gaius for these things and encouraged him to continue the same behavior. He was to send the traveling evangelists on in "a manner worthy of God" (v. 6). This means he was to do it in a way God would approve. John, in the last half of verse 6, pleads with Gaius.

> John exhorts Gaius to continue caring for the traveling messengers of the gospel of Christ. He tells him, "You will do well to send them on their way in a manner worthy of God." The phrase *you will do well* is a polite request that is similar to the expression *please.* John's instruction "to send them on their way" means that after Gaius provided lodging, he has to supply the brothers with food, money, and possibly travel companions for their journey (see Titus 3:13). John adds that Gaius must do so "in a manner worthy of God." That is, he ought to provide these services in such a manner that God receives praise (compare Col. 1:10; Phil. 1:27; 1 Thess. 2:12).[6]

Those whom Gaius had helped and whom he was urged to continue to help by giving them provisions as they went on their way deserved all he could do for them. They had gone out "for the sake of the Name, accepting nothing from the Gentiles" (v. 7). Here John explains further why Gaius was to continue his good work based on truth and love.

The people Gaius assisted were of a special class. They left their roles in life and gave themselves to God's work. They went out "for the sake of the Name" (v. 7). "Just conceivably this could be an allusion to the name of God. But almost certainly the reference is to the name of Jesus; in which case this becomes the only occasion throughout 3 John when the Son is mentioned."[7]

By supporting God's special servants, one becomes a fellow worker with them (v. 8). The same idea was expressed in 2 John 1:11 of those who receive and welcome false teachers. In that case there is participation in their evil deeds. Great care was therefore to be taken in the relationships that both the local church at large and Gaius as an individual formed.

Study Questions

1. Summarize as best as is possible what we know of Gaius.
2. Is John advocating a "prosperity gospel" when he writes, "you may prosper" (v. 2)?
3. What does John mean when he speaks of "walking in truth" (v. 3)?

4. What, can we gather, was the task of these "strangers" that Gaius was helping?

5. What does verse 8 say to us, the Church, today?

CHAPTER 21

The Response of Diotrephes to Truth
3 John 1:9-11

Preview:

John addresses a problem the church is having with a contrary leader named Diotrephes, who accuses with "wicked words" and puts out of the church those he dislikes.

Gaius's response to truth was to walk in it, to live according to it, to not just believe it but obey it as well. Diotrephes also responded to truth but in a totally opposite way. He rejected the truth, as his behavior demonstrates.

Simon Kistemaker writes:

We know little about Diotrephes. His name means "foster child of Zeus," which suggests that he is of Greek descent. He is a leader within the local church and turns his leadership position to selfish advantage. John writes that Diotrephes "loves to be first." Instead of serving the church, this proud person is egotistic and refuses to recognize superior authority. He himself desires to rule the church, Accordingly, Diotrephes rejects the apostolic supremacy of John. He acts contrary to the injunction of Jesus, "Whoever wants to become great among you must be your servant, and whoever wants to be first must be your slave" (Matt. 20:26-27). Incidentally, even though John introduces himself as "the elder" (v. 1), he exercises authority of a level higher than that of an elder.[1]

This man, Diotrephes, loved "to be first among them." He did not accept what John told him—the truth (v. 9). John wrote a letter to the church seeking to show them and Diotrephes the error of his way. This was not an inspired letter such as was written to Gaius (3 John). It was lost or possibly even destroyed by Diotrephes. The truth John conveyed in this letter was not received by Diotrephes, which means that Diotrephes also rejected John's authority. Diotrephes was a proud man who loved to be first in everything; he was a law unto himself.

The apostle John is sending the missionaries to the churches to care for them, not that the churches would pamper the missionaries. Diotrephes is mentioned again as the deceiver, and there is the ongoing warning against him and others like him. The deceivers are not to be brought into the house, or be greeted. The true and faithful missionaries only are to be treated properly and accepted into the homes. To great the heretics or have fellowship with them is forbidden. The true missionaries are co-workers for the truth.

Gaius and Diotrephes were likely both members of the same local church. There is no evidence of any theological heresy causing a conflict in the church; the problem was simply a matter of personal ambition. John's approach to this problem was to go directly to the offender by means of his church. When that effort was thwarted, he then warned and instructed Gaius and revealed his own plans to deal with Diotrephes (v. 10).

"If I come" (v. 10) represents a hypothetical case. Perhaps John's health due to his age was such that he was not sure he could come. If he were to go to Gaius's church, John leaves no doubt that his action would be strong and decisive. He does not threaten to interfere with local church affairs, but he does promise to bring before the assembly the sins of Diotrephes. John must have believed in the local church's authority to carry out its own business without any assistance from outside authority.

It sounds suspicious that Diotrephes had convinced many in the church that he was right and John was wrong. John levels a fourfold accusation against him. He "unjustly accuse[s] us with wicked words." "Neither does he . . . receive the brethren." He "forbids those who desire to do so." And he "puts them out of the church" (v. 10). Add these to Diotrephes' refusal to heed John's counsel in the letter he had sent to the church (v. 9). Precisely how this man put out of the church those who helped the itinerant missionaries is not revealed. The meaning of the expression seems to be that he worked behind the scenes and convinced enough of the members to carry out the deed.

The fourth and fifth steps taken by Diotrephes illustrate the thoroughness of his rejection of the presbyter's influence. He hinders any who wish to welcome the brothers and expels from the church those who do so. . . .

The fact that the members of this Johannine church can be forced to reverse their custom of hospitality to visiting brothers and thus move against the impetus of the commandment shows Diotrephes' power.[2]

In summary of verses 9 and 10, we may say that Diotrephes rejected the truth and sought to suppress it. We have reason to think he was not a believer. R. C. H. Lenski raises an interesting question about Diotrephes:

Had Diotrephes thrown Gaius out of the church? These present tenses say what Diotrephes is engaged in doing; they do not say that he accomplished his will in every case. He certainly kept his own house closed. Very likely, too, in most cases he succeeded in enforcing his demand that the rest also do so. He attained so much that John could send no missionaries to the congregation as such to be lodged with various members. We see this from the fact that John sends his missionaries directly to Gaius. Diotrephes would create so much trouble in the congregation that taking care of John's missionaries on the part of the congregation was practically at an end.[3]

For the third time in this short letter, John refers to his original reader, Gaius, as "beloved" (v. 11 cf. vv. 2 and 5). In this instance he does so to introduce an exhortation that has both a negative and a positive side. The exhortation centers in the word *imitate* or *follow*. It is a present imperative in a prohibition, "Do not imitate" (v. 11). The present tense would give the idea of continuing what was at the time going on.[4] The positive side of the exhortation is to imitate "what is good." John then adds the phrase, "The one who does good is of God; the one who does evil has not seen God" (v. 11). John Stott's comment on this is appropriate.

This is the moral test which is often applied in the First Epistle (e.g., 2:3–6, 28, 29; 3:4–10; 5:18). Indeed an illustration of each of the three tests is given in this Epistle—truth (verses 3, 4), love (6) and now goodness (11). The true Christian may be described both as being of God (cf. 1 Jn. 4:4, 6) and as having seen God (cf. 1 Jn. 3:6). Birth of God and the vision of God are to some extent equivalent. He who has been born of God has come, with the inner eye of faith, to see God.[5]

Kistemaker concludes:

"Anyone who does what is good is from God." The person who continually obeys God's precepts has his spiritual origin in God and is his child. How do we know the children of God? In his first epistle John gives the norm for determining the difference between the children of God and the children of the devil: "Anyone who does not do what is right is not a child of God" (3:10). Therefore, anyone who continues to do evil, for example, Diotrephes, has not seen or known God (compare 1 John 3:6). The believer sees God in Jesus Christ. As Jesus told Philip, "Anyone who has seen me has seen the Father" (John 14:9; also see 1:18). When a Christian sees God, he has fellowship with him through Jesus Christ (1 John 1:3).[6]

Everyone agrees that John had Diotrephes in view when he set forth this exhortation. He was also exhorting Gaius not to follow this man's example. Gaius was well loved in his church and acted honorably in his service for the Lord. John was trying to urge him to act with generous and open hospitality. The apostle also draws the line straight in this verse 11. Those who do good are from God, but the one who does evil has not seen God, and certainly does not know him.

Study Questions

1. Summarize as best as is possible what we know of Diotrephes.

2. Contrast the information on Diotrephes from question 1 with what we know about Gaius.

CHAPTER 22

The Response of Demetrius to Truth
3 John 1:12-14

Preview:

John commends one named Demetrius, who receives a good testimony from everyone, and closes by expressing a hope that he can visit Gaius and impart "many things" in person rather than by letter.

The apostle John now gives favorable commendation to Demetrius. It is only from these verses here that we know anything about him. For whatever reason, the apostle considered it important for Gaius to know and to trust him. Clearly, Gaius upheld all that John was saying and doing for the sake of the gospel.

How could the truth speak well of Demetrius? Many believe that John sees here the truth personified. If this is right, then truth stands for the Lord, for Christ and the gospel, and even revelation in general. But many think the truth of the gospel within Demetrius is in view. Just as Gaius, Demetrius is "walking in the truth" and his life seems to be lining up with his profession of faith. As Paul would say, he is "walking in the Spirit." As John would say, he is living he life of love! The statement, "and you know that our testimony is true" seems to refer to John 21:24.

In sharp contrast to Diotrephes' response, Demetrius gave testimony to the truth. The result of Demetrius's response was selflessness and praise from God. We know very little about this man, but what we do know is praiseworthy. He "received a good testimony from everyone" (v. 12). His testimony was confirmed by the truth itself—"and from the truth" (v. 12). John and others also gave testimony concerning him—"and we also bear witness" (v. 12).

When John thought about Diotrephes, he thought of the evil deeds Diotrephes committed. When he thought of good deeds, he thought about Demetrius.

> The objective Truth of God, which is the divine rule of the walk of all believers, gives a good testimony to him who really walks in the truth. This witness lies in the accordance of his walk with the requirement of God's truth. It was the mirror in which the walk of Demetrius was reflected; and his form, thus seen in the mirror of God's Truth, in which the perfect form of Christ is held up to us (1 John 2:6; 3:3, 16), appeared in the likeness of Christ; so that the mirror itself seemed to place in a clear light his Christian virtue and uprightness, and thus to bear witness to him.[1]

Conclusion

John planned to visit Gaius "shortly" (v. 14). For this reason he did not write a longer letter. The other things could wait until he saw Gaius "face to face" (v. 14). Gaius was going to have to deal with Demetrius and all the trouble he caused in the house church. He needed John's "Peace be to you" (v. 14).

A final exhortation was given. Gaius was to greet all "the friends by name" (v. 14). Just as Christ the Chief Shepherd calls His own by name (John 10:3), so was Gaius, an undershepherd, to do so.

Simon Kistemaker comments:

> After writing the address, John praises Gaius, whom he calls his "dear friend." He expresses the wish that Gaius may receive physical as well as spiritual blessings. John commends him, for he has received a report about the faithfulness of Gaius to the truth, especially in showing hospitality to traveling missionaries. John encourages him to continue to do so.

> John informs Gaius about the character and reprehensible deeds of Diotrephes, who has slandered the apostle and hindered the members of the congregation in providing food and shelter for the missionaries. He instructs Gaius not to follow this bad example, but rather to imitate that which is good. Thus, he mentions Demetrius, who has a good report in the church.

> The epistle has a brief conclusion with the information of a forthcoming visit of John and greetings from friends to friends.[2]

Study Questions

1. Summarize as best as is possible what we know of Demetrius.

2. As a point of interest, how many times in this short letter does John use the word *truth?*

3. What overall spiritual impression do you have from reading and studying this short letter?

SECTION 4

Courage to Stand

The Book of Jude

CHAPTER 23

Background of Jude

Author

Who is this Jude? Since he is the brother of James, who is named as one of the sons born to Joseph and Mary after Jesus was born (Matt. 13:55), Jude also is a half-brother of the Lord. Humbly he does not flaunt his relationship to Christ. Rather, he prefers that his readers know him as "a bond-servant of Jesus Christ, and brother of James" (v. 1). Like Paul and Peter, Jude considers himself Jesus Christ's slave.

> We know practically nothing about the life of this Jude. He was apparently one of the younger brothers of Jesus (Matt. 13:55; Mark 6:3). With the rest of the brothers he seems to have disbelieved in Jesus before the resurrection (John 7:3–8); but he was apparently convinced of the deity of Jesus by that event and is found with the other brothers and Mary in the upper room after the ascension (Acts 1:14). He was married and apparently traveled a good deal, taking his wife with him on his travels (1 Cor. 9:3). He probably confined his ministry to Israel, carrying out the general agreement of the Jerusalem Council (Gal. 2:9). Hegesippus tells us that near the end of Domitian's reign (c. A.D. 95), two grandsons of Jude, farmers, were brought before the emperor on the charge that they were descendants of David and were Christians. When Domitian learned that they were poor and saw their horny hands, he dismissed them as harmless Jews. It really does seem as if a forger would have selected the name of some more outstanding personage if he wanted to gain prestige for his Epistle.[1]

We do not know for certain when Jude wrote this book, the last of the General Epistles. Nor is to whom he wrote stated. R. C. H. Lenski argues convincingly that Jude wrote after Peter wrote his epistles—A.D. 63–66.

The fact that Jude uses Second Peter, or that Second Peter uses Jude, is obvious. The former is the case. Peter prophesies: "Also among you there *shall be* pseudo-teachers, such as," etc., (2 Pet. 2:1), "there *shall come* mockers" (2 Pet. 3:3). Jude 4 records the fulfillment of this prophecy: "there *did creep in covertly some men,* those who long ago *have* been written down in advance for this sentence." The kind of men, who, according to Peter, shall come, who, according to Jude, *did* actually come, Jude describes in terms that are taken from Peter, to which he adds expressions of his own. So Jude also repeats some of the divine judgments on the ungodly that were referred to by Peter and adds still others of the same kind. Jude rests on Second Peter.[2]

Parallels Between Jude and 2 Peter

Most scholars hold that Jude comes after 2 Peter as shown. Kistemaker writes:

Jude's letter is strikingly similar to Peter's second epistle. Although the parallelism is evident especially in the second chapter of 2 Peter, an examination reveals that neither of the two writers slavishly copied material. This is a list of parallel passages:[3]

Parallel Passages—Jude and 2 Peter		
Jude 1:4	godless men who deny the sovereign Lord	2 Peter 2:1
Jude 1:6	angels held in darkness for judgment	2 Peter 2:4
Jude 1:7	Sodom and Gomorrah burned to ashes	2 Peter 2:6
Jude 1:8	these men arrogantly slander celestial beings	2 Peter 2:10
Jude 1:9	Michael did not bring a slanderous accusation	2 Peter 2:11
Jude 1:10	these blasphemers are like brute beasts	2 Peter 2:12
Jude 1:11	they have followed the way of Balaam	2 Peter 2:15
Jude 1:12	clouds without rain, driven by a storm	2 Peter 2:17
Jude 1:13	blackest darkness is reserved for them	2 Peter 2:17
Jude 1:16	they lust, boast, and flatter	2 Peter 2:18
Jude 1:17	the apostles of our Lord foretold	2 Peter 3:2
Jude 1:18	in the last days scoffers will come	2 Peter 3:3

On the relationship of Jude to 2 Peter, A. T. Robertson comments:

Beyond a doubt one of these Epistles was used by the other, as one can see by comparing particularly Jude 3-18 and 2 Peter 2:1-18. . . . Scholars are greatly divided on this point, and in our state of knowledge it does not seem possible to reach a solid conclusion. The probability is that not much time elapsed between them. Mayor devotes a whole chapter to the discussion of the relation between 2 Peter and Jude and reaches the conclusion "that in Jude we have the first thought, in Peter the second thought." That is my own feeling, but it is all so Subjective that I have no desire to urge the point unduly.[4]

Peter predicted the appearance of false teachers (2 Pet. 2:1; 3:3). Jude wrote that they had already come; they were present among God's people (Jude 1:4). Lenski adds, "If all this does not mean that Jude wrote *after* Peter, yea wrote to the *same* people at a time when Peter's prophecy had been fulfilled, when the men who Peter said *shall* steal in heresies *did* themselves steal in—pray what does it mean?"[5]

The church of Jesus Christ is able to learn a lot about what Jude says of himself. As already mentioned, he makes two important claims. By seeing himself as Christ's servant (bondslave) he places the Lord front and forward before any family relation. The apostles Peter (2 Pet. 1:1) and Paul (Rom. 1:1) gloried in their servitude under Jesus. And both Jude and James seem to likewise call themselves His servants, though they also had positions as half-brothers. This stands out as a stark contrast as how these relations went before the Lord's resurrection when His brothers did not believe in him, and even thought He was crazy (John 7:5; Mark 3:21, 31). Since trusting in Christ, James steps forward to make it his life's aim to be at the disposal of Jesus the Messiah!

When Jude calls himself the brother of James this can mean only one person, the beloved apostle, the Lord's brother, and the leader of the church at Jerusalem. While it is true that many others labeled Jude the "brother of the Lord" (1 Cor. 9:5), he really seemed to want to be known simply as the "brother of James" and "the servant of Jesus Christ." This would be a mark of humility. Jude does not wish to set himself forth in a factual but, maybe to him, an undo way.

Conservative scholarship dates the letter between A.D. 70 and 80.

The Original Recipients of the Letter

Henry Thiessen says this about the destination of the letter:

It is impossible to determine with certainty the locality for which the Epistle was intended. Palestine, Asia Minor, and Alexandria have been suggested, but the letter offers no real clue as to its destination. Jude merely says: "To them that are called, beloved in God the Father, and kept for Jesus Christ" (v. 1). He admonishes them to build themselves up in their most holy faith (v. 20). The persons addressed were Christians, then; but they apparently embraced all Christians, whether Jews or Gentiles, whether inside or outside Palestine. The contents are such as would chiefly interest Jewish Christians, and the Epistle may have been intended primarily for those in Palestine and adjoining countries; but the address does not limit the message to them. All Christians are before the writer's mind. The evils are those opposed in 2 Peter, and it does not seem as if both would write to the same people, especially not if Jude is somewhat dependent upon 2 Peter. It seems more likely that Jude was meant for the same people as those for whom the author's brother James wrote his Epistle.[6]

It is generally thought that Jude intended his letter for Christian Jews from the area of Judah. Jude assumed his readers would understand his references to the Old Testament events and people as well as to the extrabiblical literature he referenced. Beyond this, we have no basis for being more specific.

The idea that Jews were intended as his audience seems to be strengthened in his opening verse 1: "to those who are the called, beloved in God the Father, and kept for Jesus Christ." This is but one of Jude's triads in this short epistle that seems to echo the Old Testament. "Called, loved and kept" may be derived from the Servant Songs in Isaiah where Israel is so described by God. The Lord lovingly calls His people by their name (45:3b), loves them (63:9), and keeps them "in perfect peace" (26:3). Jude is not making such reference to call the church saints part of ancient Israel. He is simply referring to great uplifting thoughts from the pages of Isaiah that would bring comfort to his Jewish brethren.

Thesis

The thesis or design of the book hangs on verse 3: "Beloved, while I was making every effort to write you about our common salvation, I felt the necessity to write to you appealing that you contend earnestly for the faith which was once delivered to the saints." From this "common salvation" will flow Jude's arguments, i.e., the doctrines that have to do with salvation which were held by most everyone in the newly founded Christian churches. Jude wishes to show the reasons for this earnest contending for the faith. He wants to restate the truths that were originally delivered once to the believers. Now those truths are under attack, with heresy and false teachers roaming abroad throughout the realms where the churches have been established. Jude will show that these men are crafty and clever, who have appeared almost silently but suddenly in the congregations. Though they profess simple belief in Christ, they had perverted the truth, spreading corruption, and undermining biblical faith. Confusion was running rampant. From this setting, Jude develops his Purpose for writing.

Purpose

Jude's purpose in writing is made very clear. He wrote to warn his readers about false teaching and to encourage defense of "the faith which was once for all delivered to the saints" (v. 3).

Seeds of the antinomian form of Gnosticism were beginning to sprout with the belief that spirit was good and matter was evil. This led to license to sin and freedom to pursue anything the spirit desired. Lawlessness characterized those who subscribed to this philosophy of life that was contrary to the teaching of Scripture.

Jude's style of writing deserves comment. He uses figures of speech—false teachers were hidden reefs, waterless clouds, autumn trees, wild waves, and wandering stars (vv. 12–13). Triads mark the letter of Jude. One example is his reference to his original readers as "called, beloved . . . and kept" (v. 1).

The emerging picture of the world of Gnosticism is very complicated. Generally speaking, the Gnostic world-view was hostile toward the world and all worldly ties. From this perspective, Gnosticism branched into ascetic and libertine divisions. For God (who is absolutely transmundane) but from the Archons (or the demiurges) who are related to this world. Salvation . . . involves the intentional violations of the rules of the Archons. Gnosticism also could cause a nihilism. In some systems, the Gnostics despaired of this world to such an extent that body and soul were meaningless. . . . Against this kind of thinking, Jude's strong polemic becomes understandable. . . . Jude's vehement opposition to this kind of error was justified in the light of the significant issues that were involved.[7]

The Canonicity of Jude

While Martin Luther accepted the book as canonical, he had little compliments to give it. This is surprising because it is critical of false religion and heresy he was fighting in the German Reformation. He seems to be giving the epistle a positive note when he wrote that it was "an epistle against our clergy, bishops, priests and monks." He said about Jude:

The authorship of this epistle is attributed to the holy apostle Jude—the brother of the two apostles and James the Less and Simon. They were his brothers by the sister of the mother of Christ, who is called Mary (the wife) of James and Cleopas, as we read in Mark 6:3; 16:1. However, this epistle does not seem to be from one of the first apostles; for in it the author speaks of the apostles, as if he were their junior, having lived long after them. In it is nothing special except it refers to the Second Epistle of Peter from which it has taken nearly all its words, and on the whole it is nothing else than an epistle against our clergy, bishops, priests and monks.[8]

Kistemaker further notes about Luther:

In the preface to his New Testament edition of 1522, Martin Luther lists all twenty-seven books by name. The first twenty-three he gives sequential numbers, but the last four are numberless. They are Hebrews, James, Jude, and Revelation. Luther maintains that Jude's epistle is an abstract of 2 Peter and therefore is unnecessary among the New Testament epistles. . . . His fellow Reformer John Calvin accepted Jude because the early church placed it among the canonical books of the New Testament.[9]

On the subject of Jude and the New Testament canon, Calvin wrote:

Though there was a dispute among the ancients concerning this Epistle, yet as the reading of it us useful, and as it contains nothing inconsistent with the purity of apostolic doctrine, and was received as authentic formerly, by some of the best, I willingly add it to the others.[10]

Why was Jude originally put on hold as an apostolic writing? Some have said it's because of its brevity, and its allusions to the Jewish Apocrypha writings of I Enoch, the Testament of Moses, and the Assumption of Moses. And since it has parallels with 2 Peter, many seem to regard it simply as a copy of that book. But numerous references to Jude found at the end of the first century and from the second century make it clear that the church at large had no problem with its canonicity. The Muratorian Canon (AD 175) gives the first witness and mentions the book by name: "An epistle of Jude and two with the title John are accepted in the catholic [apostolic] Church."[11] The book is also mentioned in the writings of Tertullian (AD 200).

More on the Apocrypha quotes later, but it may be noted here:

There are some things to be noted about how Jude quotes these religious writings, that may have contained some truth, yet were not considered inspired. First, Jude doesn't use any statements of authority in quoting, such as "It is written." Or, "the Word of God says." When he mentions the rebuke against the devil, "the Lord rebuke you," Jude is using this clause, taken from Zechariah 3:2, as a principle way to refute Satan. Thus, his entire approach to these quotes is but illustrative rather than authoritative.[12]

On the canonicity of Jude, Lenski well summarizes:

Regarding Jude as well as Second Peter, Bigg supplies the *testimonia veterum* which indicate that Jude's epistle was known as far back as the beginning of the second century. Small as this is and not of general interest we certainly can expect no more. In his commentary on Matt. 13:55, Origen remarks: "Jude, the Lord's brother, wrote an epistle of few lines but full of the strong words of heavenly grace." Eusebius classes Jude among the antilegomena because it was not written by an apostle. The oldest manuscripts of the Syriac Peshito omit Jude. Jerome accepts it but remarks: *a plerisque rejicitur*. Jude is, however, in the canon of the Synod of Laodicea (363) and in that of Carthaginia (397) and has maintained its position ever since.

The men of the Reformation voiced doubts as to its canonical standing, and since then various commentators have for various reasons shared these doubts. The critics claim that Jude is a forgery like Second Peter. Why a second-century writer should select such a minor man as Jude to forge an epistle in his name is difficult to understand. Why one forger should utilize another forger is still more incredible; which is true whether the author of Second Peter or Jude is forger number one. And both of them were not detected until modern times.[13]

Outline of Jude

I. Salutation and Warning about False Teachers (Jude 1:1-4)

    A. Salutation (Jude 1:1-2)

    B. Warning (Jude 1:3-4)

II. Explanations about False Teachers (Jude 1:5-16)

    A. Reminders of God's Certain Judgment (Jude 1:5-7)

    B. Reasons for God's Certain Judgment on False Teachers (Jude 1:8-16)

III. Exhortations and Encouragement for Believers (Jude 1:17-25)

    A. Exhortations (Jude 1:17-23)

    B. Encouragement (Jude 1:24-25)

CHAPTER 24

Salutation and Warning about False Teachers
Jude 1:1-4

Preview:
Jude writes to urge believers to "contend earnestly for the faith." He warns of some who are condemned, who turn the grace of God into licentiousness "and deny our only Master and Lord, Jesus Christ."

Salutation (Jude 1:1-2)

Jude identifies himself simply as "a bond-servant of Jesus Christ" (v. 1). John informs us that there was a time when Jesus' half-brothers, which would include Jude, did not believe in Him (John 7:5). Later, after Jesus' resurrection, they did believe on Him (Acts 1:14).

Of the siblings of Jesus, the most is known of James and Jude. James was probably with the family when they sought to see the Lord somewhere in Galilee (Matt. 12:46); as well, he went with Jesus to Capernaum (John 2:12), and later joined in the attempt to Persuade Him to go to Judea for the Feast of Tabernacles, though he did not believe in Him (John 7:3, 5, 10). When Jesus appeared to him alone after his resurrection (1 Cor. 15:7), James may first have believed in Him as Savior.

Jude was possibly here in Acts 1:14 in the upper room following Christ's ascension. He was married and apparently traveled a lot, taking his wife along (1 Cor. 9:5). Most believe he remained in Israel and carried out the agreement of the Jerusalem Council (Gal. 2:9).[1]

About Jude, Henry C. Thiessen adds:

Hegesippus tells us that near the end of Domitian's reign (C.A.D. 95), two grandsons of Jude, farmers, were brought before the emperor on the charge that they were descendants of David and were Christians. When Domitian learned that they were poor and saw their horny hands, he dismissed them as harmless Jews.[2]

Jude went out of his way not to address his readers in a manner that could be interpreted as claiming special authority. Yet he did want them to know that James, who was perhaps better known than Jude, was his brother. This is the basis for identifying him as Jesus' half-brother.

Those addressed were "the called, beloved in God the Father, and kept for Jesus Christ" (v. 1). The Father's past sovereign call, His past and present love of those called, and His present and future keeping of them are assured. In view of the major thrust of Jude's letter, the false teaching in their midst, this was indeed an encouraging word.

The God who calls and secures makes constant provision for His own. Jude's genuine love and concern for these who were hearing the apostate teaching of the false teachers are expressed in these words—*mercy, peace,* and *love* (v. 2). R. C. H. Lenski makes this observation: "The readers of Jude are suffering a terrible infliction and thus need "mercy" multiplied to them. Men are trying to destroy their relation to God in Christ, and thus they need "peace" multiplied, all that will conserve their relation to God. And thus they will need God's all-comprehending love with all its gifts."[3]

Warning (Jude 1:3–4)

The ones "beloved in God" (v. 1) are also Jude's "beloved" (v. 3). At the very outset they must know that. They also must know that Jude changed his purpose in writing to them because of a pressing need they had. They were hearing and being affected by apostate teaching. Some in their midst even may have begun to give a sympathetic ear. Therefore, rather than write to them about "our common salvation" (v. 3), he wrote words of warning. Lenski adds:

Jude says that in the midst of his plans for writing to his readers on a larger subject he all at once found himself compelled to write this letter in which he urges them to keep on contending earnestly for the faith delivered once for all to the saints. . . . News had unexpectedly reached Jude that heretics had crept into the congregations; he finds that he must act at once, and he does so by means of this letter.[4]

Jude's readers needed to "contend earnestly for the faith which was once for all delivered to the saints" (v. 3). Jude was not calling them to defend their individual faith, but the body of truth that was "once for all delivered to the saints" (v. 3), the apostolic faith. This contending for the faith was necessary because ungodly persons had crept in unnoticed and were turning the grace of God into licentiousness and denying the Lord Jesus Christ (v. 4). Jude reminds his readers that the condemnation of these apostates was revealed beforehand; they were marked out for it. This very likely refers to Old Testament (i.e., Jer. 5:13–14) and New Testament Scripture (2 Pet. 2:1–3).

Some consider the clause "marked out for this condemnation" a troubling statement. In the Greek text, "marked out" is actually a perfect passive participle of the verb "to write before" (*"prographo"*) and means that this written judgment had been recorded sometime in the past, with the action coming up to the present. Jude could mean: (1) that it was written in the Old Testament Scriptures that some like this would depart, (2) that this was recorded earlier in 2 Peter 2:3. But the expression "long beforehand" seems to rule this out, (3) that this was recorded in Enoch's prophecy, (4) that it refers metaphorically to their judgment sealed before hand in heaven, (5) that these men, though not atheists, are simply godless who pretend to know God. On this last point Kistemaker writes:

> "They are godless men, who change the grace of our God into a license for immorality." What are these intruders doing that they deserve divine condemnation? To put it in the words of Paul, "They claim to know God, but by their actions they deny him. They are detestable, disobedient and unfit for doing anything good" (Titus 1:16).
>
> Jude does not say that these men are atheists. He indicates that they slyly enter the Christian church by acknowledging the existence of God; otherwise they would be denied entrance. But their personal conduct betrays godlessness, for these men think that God's grace allows them to indulge in unbridled sexual freedom.[5]

On this verse, the old Presbyterian divine Thomas Manton notes:

> The meaning of the metaphor is to show that these decrees [against these ungodly men] are as certain and determinate as if he had a book wherein to write them. Now, these are said to be 'written before of old,' to show, that though they crept in unawares as to the church, yet not as to God; they fell under the notice of his decrees before ever they acted in this evil

way. It is further added, that they were ordained or written down in God's book, . . . 'for judgment,' or 'condemnation;' . . . The meaning of the whole is, that they were such as were left to themselves, to bring upon themselves by their own sins and errors a just condemnation.[6]

For the word "Master," Jude uses the very strong word *despotēs* that carries the ides of an absolute, all-powerful ruler. In the negative sense, the word conjures up the picture of an ill-tempered and cruel master. The word is used only five times in the New Testament in referring to either God (Acts 4:24; Rev. 6:10), or Christ (Luke 2:29; 2 Pet. 2:1; Jude 1:4). The sovereignty of the Lord is emphasized by this word. It may be applied to God and Christ as benevolent Despots! Vincent writes that, "Originally, it indicates *absolute, unrestricted* authority, so that the Greeks refused the title to any but the gods."[7]

A Summary of Jude's Doctrine of "Judgment"

Those who deny Christ are due condemnation (v. 4).

The Lord destroyed the unbelievers who came out of Egypt (v. 5).

The angels who fell are bound for judgment (v. 6).

Those who are immoral are due the punishment of eternal fire (v. 7).

The devil is due judgment (v. 9).

Revilers are to be destroyed (v. 10).

Those who have sinned after the way of Cain, the error of Balaam, and the rebellion of Korah, are to perish (v. 11).

Those who have crept into churches with their sin are reserved forever under black darkness (v. 13).

The Lord will someday come to execute judgment on the ungodly (v. 15).

The Lord will someday come to convict the ungodly of their deeds (v. 15).

Believers are to have mercy on some, snatching them from fire (vv. 22–23).

Jude predicts an increase in the denial of the faith in the last days before the rapture of the true church. Jesus warned of those in sheep's clothing who would be in reality ravenous wolves (Matt. 7:15). Paul was clear in his warning to leaders in the church at Ephesus about "savage wolves" who would come among them not sparing the flock (Acts 20:28–32). Timothy was told that "in latter times some will fall away from the faith" (1 Tim. 4:1). Peter told his readers of false prophets who would arise (2 Pet. 2:1). From all such teaching God's people are told to "avoid" such men (2 Tim. 3:5) and to not participate with such but to expose their deeds (Eph. 5:11).

The Lord Jesus can be denied in many ways apart from those things that are obviously apostate. The heretics Jude is speaking of had a certain practical denial by the life they lived. And either openly, are with subtlety, they were rejecting the deity of Christ and His sovereignty. While many believe that Gnosticism was only incipient at this stage in church history, it was growing and deeply effecting what was being taught in the churches. Part of what this belief taught was that the God of Scripture was not the highest god, or the only deity. Jesus was only a man who was baptized by the Spirit, and then the Spirit left Him at the crucifixion. The Gnostics are said to have been reckless in their charges against Jesus!

Study Questions

1. What is the evidence that shows Jude is the half-brother of Jesus?

2. Who were the original recipients of this letter?

3. What is the purpose of the letter?

4. What does Jude say that shows God's judgment is certain and will come to pass?

5. What does it mean to "turn the grace of our God into licentiousness" (v. 4)?

CHAPTER 25

Explanations about False Teachers
Jude 1:5-16

Preview:

In describing evil, Jude writes about the fallen angels, the sins of Sodom and Gomorrah, the confrontation between the archangel Michael and Satan over the body of Moses, the murder committed by Cain, the error of Balaam, and the rebellion of Korah. Jude is making the point that all evildoers are doomed and face a righteous judgment.

Reminders of God's Certain Judgment (Jude 1:5-7)

After alerting his readers to the apostate teachers among them, Jude brings to their attention how God judged others who were guilty of similar sins. First, he reminds them of apostasy in the chosen nation, Israel, and how God dealt with it (v. 5). This apostasy took place while the people were wandering in the wilderness after they had been delivered from Pharaoh's cruel hand in Egypt (Num. 14:36–37). Spies had been sent to explore the land God had promised His people. Kenneth Wuest gives a clear description of the incident and how most of the spies simply disbelieved God.

> The instance to which Jude has reference is that of the Jews, after having been convinced by the spies of the truth of God's assertion that the land of Canaan was a land flowing with milk and honey, most productive as proved by the grapes they brought out, yet refused to enter it, not trusting

God to give them the land as He said He would do. This was apostasy, sinning with the eyes wide open, and could only be dealt with by the afflic-
tion of the death penalty. That generation died a physical death in the
wilderness.[1]

The expression *you know all things once for all*, may better read *though you
once knew this.* Jude's point is that they had before been acquainted with the
story of the wilderness wandering, and they needed to be reminded afresh of
its importance in light of what was then happening in the churches. In like
manner, the present apostates are rebelling and causing doubt in the minds of
the believers.

The bearing of this fact on the case, before the mind of Jude, seems to
have been this—that, as those who had been delivered from Egypt were
afterward destroyed for their unbelief, or as the mere fact of their being
rescued did not prevent destruction from coming on them, so the fact that
these persons *seemed* to be delivered from sin, and had become professed
followers of God, would not prevent their being destroyed if they led
wicked lives.[2]

Jude's second illustration of the certainty of God's judgment upon apostasy is His punishment on the terrible sin of some of the angels who had
already followed Satan in his rebellion (v. 6). The angels who committed this
additional sin were immediately judged by being "kept in eternal bonds
under darkness for the judgment of the great day" (v. 6). Not all wicked angels
or demons are thus confined. Many are free to roam and continue to afflict
the saints of God and will do so until they will be cast into the lake of fire
along with the devil himself (Matt. 25:41; Rev. 20:10).

The Bible Knowledge Commentary makes an interesting observation
about verse 6:

Jude's source of information for this statement is debated. Some feel that
this may refer to Genesis 6:1–4, and that "the sons of God" who cohabited with "the daughters of men" on earth were the angels who left "their
positions of authority" in disobedience to God. . . . Others feel Jude was
making use of the apocryphal Book of Enoch. Since Jude did not identify
his source, any decision is only conjecture. The way Jude referred to the
angels give reason to believe that this truth was well accepted by his readers and thus needed no further explanation.[3]

Identifying the "spirits in prison" as wicked angels harmonizes well
with 2 Peter 2:4 and Jude 6. Both of these passages speak of wicked
angels who are confined until their eternal judgment. Also in both pas-

sages the sin for which they are bound was sexual, which fits with Genesis 6:1-4 and our understanding of 1 Peter 3:18-20. In 2 Peter 2:4-5 Peter associated the angels who sinned in Noah's day with the sexual immorality of Sodom and Gomorrah. Jude wrote that the angels to which he referred were "kept in eternal bonds under darkness" because they "did not keep their own domain, but abandoned their proper abode" (Jude 6). If the "sons of God" in Genesis 6 and the "spirits now in prison" in 1 Peter 3:19 are not wicked angels, we have no other explanation of why some demons are bound while others are free to roam.[4]

What sin did these demons commit which brought about this confinement in darkness until the judgment day? Jude quickly moves from this sin and judgment among angels to the sins of the people of Sodom and Gomorrah (v. 7), whose sins were sexual and going after "strange flesh" (v. 7). These words of Jude seem to support the identification of the "sons of God" in Genesis 6 as angelic beings. Peter also wrote about these same angels who sinned and were put in "pits of darkness, reserved for judgment" (2 Pet. 2:4). In the very next verse he refers to Noah and the Flood (v. 5).

These two passages, Jude 1:6 and 2 Peter 2:4, provide much help in understanding the sin described in Genesis 6:1-4. There we are told that the "sons of God" took the "daughters of men" as their wives with the resultant judgment of the global flood (Gen. 6:14-22). These angels in Jude 6 were most likely the wicked angels, or demons, who cohabited with women of the earth, and the progeny of their union were called "Nephilim . . . mighty men . . . men of renown" (Gen. 6:4).

There is controversy in Genesis 6:1-4. Some believe that the author of Genesis, Moses, is calling the righteous branch of early humanity the sons of God who came through the Seth who replaced Abel, who had been slain by Cain. The "daughters of men" then would be the earthy and ungodly branch who came through the line of Cain. Others, however, hold that the "sons of God" are fallen angels. The expression "sons of God" (*bene elohim*) has various interpretations. Harold G. Stigers does not think the sons of God are angelic beings. He writes that in the passage

> The emphasis is one of contrast: the "sons of God" stand opposed to the "daughters of men." Further light on the contrast is found in Job 1:6 where the sons of God are in contrast to Satan, and here they would be the heavenly beings, but this does not force us to conclude that the "sons of God" in Genesis 6 are angelic, for the contrast there is between human beings [such as the sons of Cain, and the sons of Seth].[5]

The Lutheran scholar H. C. Leupold holds to the same view with Stigers. He writes:

> Strictly speaking, "sons of God" is a title applied to the godly; grammatically, the very expression "sons of God" does not happen to be used in reference to them in that very form. . . . We have had no mention made of angels thus far in Genesis. We have met with other sons of the true God, in fact, the whole preceding chapter [in Genesis], even 4:25-5:32, has been concerned with them. Who will, then, be referred to here? Answer, the Sethites, without a doubt.[6]

However, Henry M. Morris holds a different view and helps in an understanding of Genesis 6:1-4. He writes:

> The actual phrase *bene elohim* is used three other times, all in the very ancient book of Job (1:6; 2:1; 38:7). There is no doubt at all that, in these passages, the meaning applies exclusively to the angels. A very similar form (*bar elohim*) is used in Daniel 3:25, and also refers either to an angel or to a theophany. The term "sons of the mighty" (*bene elim*) is used in Psalm 29:1 and also Psalm 89:6, and again refers to angels. Thus, there seems no reasonable doubt that, in so far as the language itself is concerned, the intent of the writer was to convey the thought of angels—fallen angels, no doubt, since they were acting in opposition to God's will.[7]

The third illustration of the certainty of God's judgment upon apostasy comes from the sin of the inhabitants of the cities of Sodom and Gomorrah (v. 7). These people were guilty of the same kind of sin as that committed by the angels in verse 6.

> Lot chose Sodom because it was "as the garden of the Lord (like a paradise), like the land of Egypt (so rich and fertile), well watered everywhere before the Lord destroyed Sodom and Gomorrah," Gen. 13:10. But see how this region lies now? The writer was there in 1925. Not a thing grows; not a creature lives in the waters. They are so impregnated that the hand feels the clinging salt and the other chemicals; the body of a swimmer floats. It seems almost incredible that Gen. 18:10 could at one time have been true of this blasted land.
>
> Two other cities besides Sodom and Gomorrah were destroyed, Admah and Zeboiim (Deut. 29:23; Hos. 11:8). The fifth city, Zoar, was spared, but "all the plain" was destroyed (Gen. 19:21–25). Wisdom 10:6 speaks of "Pentapolis," the five-city region. Jude does not mention the other cities because he is "harsher than Peter" but because, when one looks at what lies before the eyes, "all the plain" and the Dead Sea (Gen.

19:25) are there and not only the place where Sodom and Gomorrah once stood. Jude is exact.[8]

"Just as" (v. 7) refers back to verse 6 and the angels' sin: "Horrible licentiousness, not simply with women not their wives or in other nations, but even unnatural uses (Rom. 1:27) for which the very word *sodomy* is used (Gen. 19:4–11)."[9] "The cities around them" were Admah and Zeboiim (Deut. 29:23; Hos. 11:8). The inhabitants of these cities "indulged in gross immorality and went after strange flesh" (v. 7) "in the same way" (v. 7) as the angels in verse 6. These and the preceding two examples reveal God's certain judgment against sin.

About the sins of Sodom, as described in Genesis 19:4-5, Unger writes:

The depth of shameless depravity to which Sodom (and by clear intimation the other cities of the Pentapolis) had sunk is revealed the moral permissiveness and the so-called new morality of these last days (2 Tim. 3:1-8) have their ancient parallel. Homosexuality and sexual perversion were rampant, shameless, and ripe for judgment (cf. 13:13; 18:20; Rom. 1:27), representing present-day "new morality" in its same ancient dress.[10]

J. P. Lange quotes Wordsworth on the meaning of the final clause of Jude 7: "As Sodom and Gomorrah suffer the vengeance of a fire that consumed them finally, so that they will never be restored, as long as the world lasts, so the bodies and souls of the wicked will suffer, as long as they are capable of suffering, which, since they are immortal, will, as Tertullian says: 'be forever.'"[11]

The phrase *the punishment of eternal fire* is more than likely a reference to "the lake of fire and brimstone" where unbelievers will be sent following the great white throne judgment (Rev. 20:15). It is also the place where the beast and false prophet of the tribulation are cast to "be tormented day and night forever and ever" (v. 10). Jesus also added that the evil angels will be cast into that same place (Matt. 25:41). The demons, which are fallen angels now roaming the earth, know of this coming judgment. They asked Jesus, are you come "here to torment us before the time?" (8:29).

Reasons for God's Certain Judgment on False Teachers (Jude 1:8–16)

Jude now returns to the false teachers to whom he referred in verse 4. He related them to the wicked and immoral inhabitants of Sodom and Gomorrah—"in the same manner" (v. 8). The false teachers were beguiled by their sensual dreams, which then moved them to corrupt conduct. They "defile the flesh" (v. 8). To *defile* means to contaminate or pollute. Here it clearly speaks of corruption of physical flesh and describes licentiousness, or immoral conduct. The false teachers also "reject authority" (v. 8). The authority in view here is not just human standards and decency of conduct but divine authority as well. The context requires this. Furthermore, these false teachers "revile angelic majesties" (v. 8). The Israelites described in verse 5 had done the same. The angels who sinned (v. 6) also had committed this sin against God and His divine order, as had the inhabitants of Sodom and Gomorrah (v. 7). Thus, Jude is likening the behavior of the false teachers to the three groups in verses 5, 6, and 7.

How dare the false teachers show such contempt and irreverence for God and His angelic messengers! (2 Pet. 2:10). Even the archangel Michael did not do this. Instead, when he disputed with the devil about the body of Moses, he turned the devil over to God for His rebuke (v. 9). The current craze among some evangelicals today of binding Satan is in flagrant violation of the teaching here.

Where does Jude get his information about the struggle between Michael and Satan over the body of Moses? There is much controversy about this. Many believe it comes from the Pseudepigrapha ("false writing") known as the *Assumption of Moses.* The Old Testament Pseudepigrapha writings were written in the general era of "the birth of Christ (200 B.C. to 200 A.D.)."[12] In the *Assumption of Moses* fragment, the sentence about Moses' death the fragile paper is partly destroyed and broken off. It is therefore not clear whether Jude's statement comes from that document. "In the present case the date of the *Assumption [of Moses]* is still debated; no one can be sure Jude ever saw the *Assumption.* Scholars have drawn more than one hasty conclusion of this kind. [For example], Where did Paul obtain the names of the Egyptian sorcerers, Jannes and Jambres (2 Tim. 3:8)?"[13] It still must be remembered that it is not clear what the *Assumption* actually said. The real issue has to do with the doctrines of inspiration and inerrancy. If Jude and the other books of the New Testament are inspired by the Spirit of God, what Jude writes is true, no matter what the source. But again, Jude could simply be using this story as an illustration of the great cosmic struggle between the Lord and Satan. However, the "illustration" theory has the least credence.

What claim had Satan on the body of Moses, or for that matter, on any human body?

Obviously [Satan] was opposed to the secret burial of it, most likely because the Israelites would have embalmed it and turned it into an object of worship. However, we must give them credit, for not making the bones of Joseph an idol, for though they carried them with them, they apparently did nothing other than bury them as he requested them to do. Had they known of the whereabouts of the body of Moses, they would have been anxious to carry it over with them into the land.[14]

Jude introduces a contrast in verse 10. The false teachers are contrasted with Michael and his approach to Satan. They, the false teachers, "revile" the things they do not even understand, and they behave like "unreasoning animals" (v. 10). By this kind of behavior, they are being brought to ruin and corruption. In contrast, Michael acknowledged his own limitations and God's sovereign hand and turned Satan over to Him for disposition. It seems abundantly clear that Jude wrote with full knowledge of Peter's second letter and even may have used it as he wrote (cf. 2 Pet. 2:4–7).

Jude's words could not be any stronger. He writes with powerful arguments as to the end of these deceivers. "To revile" is weak, and so is "to rail," as is found in some other versions. The Greek verb is *blasphēmeō* with the strongest emphasis meaning "to slander." These men blaspheme the "glories" and the very attributes of the Lord Jesus Himself! What "they do not understand" shows their lack of common intelligence (1 Cor. 2:14), but mainly illustrates that they are without spiritual sense. Spiritual truth is beyond them, and when confronted with divine knowledge and wisdom, they scoff, mock, and blaspheme (Matt. 7:6). Satan himself drives them to throw their blasphemous ideas against the holy "things" of God. On "unreasoning animals" Lenski writes:

> "What thins on the other hand, physically, as the irrational animals (they are), they do understand" are, of course, not spiritual things, those referred to in the first clause, but what these unspiritual fellows can grasp "physically," with their animal senses as the irrational animals that they are. These they do understand . . . , for it takes only natural and not spiritual ability to do that. These things they likewise blaspheme. Their profanity is so senseless. Jude makes a striking turn that is similar to that made by Peter: "in connection with these things they perish," i.e., go to ruin like the unbelieving Israelites, like the rebel angels, like Sodom, etc.[15]

Jude uses another triad in verse 11. The false teachers the believers were to oppose by contending for the faith are likened to "the way of Cain," "the error of Balaam," and "the rebellion of Korah" (v. 11). Jude introduced these comparisons with a strong denunciation of the false teachers: "Woe to them!" Cain committed the first murder in the Bible. He killed his brother Abel because Abel's deeds were good and acceptable but Cain's were neither good nor acceptable (Gen. 4:4–5, 9; 1 John 3:12). The false teachers in like manner cared not at all for the spiritual welfare of those they were deceiving.

Michael Green comments on Jude's second comparison, Balaam's error:

It was Balaam who involved Israel in the immorality and idolatry at Baal-Peor (Num. 31:16). No doubt he told the Israelites, whom he had three times found himself unable to curse, that they were so firmly ensconced in the favour of the Almighty that nothing could affect their standing with Him. They could sin with impunity. Thus he led them into the *error* of fornication and the denial of Yahweh's sovereign claims through submission to other, inferior deities. This is what the false teachers seem to have done.[16]

Third, like Korah, these false teachers rebelled against God and God's servants in the local church (cf. Numbers 16). They made a concerted effort to set themselves up as superiors to the God-appointed leadership.

Besides making a comparison about rebellion against God's appointed leaders in the church, what else could Jude have in mind about the insurrection of Korah against Moses? Looking at the story in Numbers 16, there may be some important hints. Ego, ambition, along with a desire for just plain raw temporal power, could have also driven Korah to rebel. Harrison writes:

Moses discerned correctly the real motive for Korah's rebellion. Korah wanted a popular election to be held for the office of high priest with himself as a candidate. In his view he was the only suitable person for that exalted function. To set Korah's position in Israel in proper perspective. Moses pointed out the great privilege of his having been called to serve God in the ministry of the sanctuary. Moses evidently perceived that this status did not satisfy Korah's ambitions, however, and for this reason he questioned him directly on the matter of his desire to be high priest in Israel, without receiving any apparent rebuttal.[17]

Jude makes the connection of rebellion against God's Word and against His authority from these three Old Testament historic events. To the rebels in the churches, Jude uses verse 11 to make the case for their coming destruction. He sums up: "Woe to them!," they rush headlong into error and will "perish" as happened "in the rebellion of Korah."

"These men" (v. 12) refers back to "certain persons have crept in unnoticed" (v. 4). From verse 12 through verse 16 Jude uses very picturesque language to describe them. The false teachers were like treacherous "hidden reefs in your love feasts" (v. 12). In the early days of the church, the love feast was the setting for and a major part of the observance of the Lord's Table. These love feasts sometimes became occasions of greed and disorder and even immorality (cf. 1 Cor. 11:20–22). The false teachers, Jude declared, were like danger hidden in the water and would bring about spiritual shipwreck. They must have taken part in the communion service and that "without fear" (v. 12).

The comparison with "hidden reefs" is the first of another list of six of Jude's comparisons. The last one is in verse 16. The second comparison of the false teachers is to "clouds without water" (v. 12). Clouds hide the sun. These teachers hid the truth from the people and replaced it with falsehood. They were just like clouds that promise rain but fail to produce.

Third, the false teachers are like barren fruit trees, "autumn trees without fruit, doubly dead, uprooted" (v. 12). When these trees should have had fruit in the fall, they had only leaves. "At all events, these teachers had barren lives, when they should have been fruitful. They were like the barren fig tree of Jesus' parable (Luke 13:6–9)."[18]

Fourth, "wild waves of the sea casting up their own shame like foam" (v. 13) describes what the false teachers do produce in contrast to the earlier metaphors. They, like the waves, bring up all kinds of worthless things in their teaching. Shameful behavior marks these teachers. Jude likely had Isaiah 57:20 in mind: "But the wicked are like the tossing sea, for it cannot be quiet, and its waters toss up refuse and mud."

"Wandering stars for whom the black darkness has been reserved forever" (v. 13) is Jude's next characterization of the false teachers. Pretending to be lights with clear understanding of truth, the false teachers whom Jude is castigating are actually those for whom "the black darkness has been reserved forever." It seems that Jude is here thinking of the same kind of judgment to come upon the fallen angels of verse 6. They too are "under darkness for the judgment of the great day" (v. 6). Peter, writing earlier about the same angelic sin, said the sinning angels were in "pits of darkness, reserved for judgment" (2 Pet. 2:4).

Before giving his final description of the false teachers as "grumblers" certain to be judged by God, Jude refers to a prophecy given by Enoch (v. 14) to illustrate his point. He quotes from the noncanonical book of the prophet Enoch mentioned in the Bible (Gen. 5:19–24; cf. Heb. 11:5–6). Jude's use of the noncanonical source does not mean the entire source is inspired but only that which the Spirit of God directed Jude to include. The point of its inclusion is to emphasize the certainty of God's judgment to come upon the false teachers about whom Jude was warning.

There is nothing worse than for people to complain about their lot in life, but these men are doing more. They are repining, complaining, finding fault with their allotments under the providence of God. It is easy to compare one's case with someone else. It is then easy to blame God for not having made the circumstance different.

The poor complain that they are not rich like others; the sick that they are not well; the enslaved that they are not free; the bereaved that they are deprived of friends; the ugly that they are not beautiful; those in humble life that their lot was not cast among the great. . . . The virtue that is opposed to this is *contentment*—a virtue of inestimable value.[19]

Kistemaker well sums up Jude's indictment and descriptions:[20]

1. "These men are grumbles." These men, he intimates, give vent to their discontent by complaining not against men but against God.

2. "Faultfinders." They bemoan the place God has given them in life.

3. "They follow their own desires." By adding the qualifying adjective *evil*, Jude rules out the possibility of interpreting the word *desires* in a favorable sense. He is referring to physical lust that reveals itself in unlawful craving.

4. "They boast about themselves." Literally, Jude says, "And their mouth speaks haughty words." They utter arrogant speech that they are unable to confirm.

5. "[They] flatter others for their own advantage." These godless men are showing partiality to gain profits for themselves.

These men seem also to be loud, braggarts, full of themselves, impressed with their own thoughts, prepared to curry favor with others for their own gains, and able to easily take advantage of anyone.

As the fear of God drives out the fear of man, so defiance of God tends to put man in His place, as the chief source of good or evil to his fellows. At the end of all the thunderbolts which Jude has unleashed upon these folk from the armoury of God, we find them at the mercy of their own fears of what men will do to them. They are indeed cut down to size.[21]

With searing words, Luther concludes about this section of verses, that these evil men

have applied all their teaching to the externals and have carried on such a child's play and fool's work that they held it to be a great sin if anyone did not share their views. Therefore Jude puts it well, that they put a mask upon all their doings and have that alone before their eyes. Hence no one knows anything of faith, of love nor of the cross. Then the average person thus plays the monkey and the fool, and turns all his property over to them, as if they were devoting it to the true service of God; that is, they keep up a fine appearance, for the sake of their own advantage.[22]

Study Questions

1. What does Jude mean when he says that his audience knows "all things once for all" (v. 5)?

2. How do the angels in verse 6 line up with those of Genesis 6 and 2 Peter 2?

3. Where else is Michael the archangel mentioned in Scripture? What is his importance in the Bible?

4. What does verse 9 tell us about the position of Satan in the angelic hierarchy?

5. What was the "error of Balaam"?

6. Who was Korah, and what was his sin?

CHAPTER 26

Exhortations and Encouragement for Believers
Jude 1:17-25

Preview:
Jude warns believers in Christ to stay "in the love of God," and to wait eagerly for the mercy of Christ that leads to eternal life. When possible, "have mercy on some, who are doubting; save others, snatching them out of the fire."

Exhortations (Jude 1:17-23)

There is a great similarity between verses 17-18 and 2 Peter 3:1-3. The subjects are the same in that they follow the description of the false and heretical teachers against whom the apostle Jude is warning. These men are dangerous and could mislead whole churches into error. When Jude begs his readers to recall the words of the apostles, he is not inferring that he is not one. He is speaking of what was past. He is referring to the "other apostles," i.e., the twelve that had a special commission of the Lord when He was with them. "Or, it might be that he meant also to include himself among them, and to speak of the apostles collectively, without particularly specifying himself."[1]

Jude rather abruptly turns his attention to the believers whom he was addressing and away from the false teachers about whom he was warning. From the reminder from Enoch, Jude now turns to "the apostles of our Lord Jesus Christ" (v. 17). The readers must not forget these but "remember the words that were spoken beforehand" by them. The previous verses, 5–16, called for remembrance about false teachers. Here in verses 17–23 Jude calls for remembrance of earlier teaching of the truth.

The readers should not have been surprised about the presence of false teachers, for they had been warned (v. 18; cf. vv. 4, 16; 2 Pet. 3:3–4).

> The false teachers were claiming to be so Spirit-filled that there was no room for law in their Christian lives. They claimed that grace was so abundant that their sin (if so it must be called) provided greater occasion for it (cf. v. 4). They claimed that the salvation of the soul is what matters, and that what a man does with his body is immaterial, for it is bound to perish. Those who fussed about sexual purity seemed to them astonishingly naive.[2]

The false teachers were divisive, "worldly-minded," and "devoid of the Spirit" (v. 19). Jude's assessment of them is that they were unregenerate. Many were following these false teachers just as Peter said they would (2 Pet. 2:2). They were following after their natural depraved instincts.

In verse 19, "cause divisions" seems reminiscent of Paul's indictment against the Corinthians who promoted quarrels and divisions (1 Cor. 1:11-13). "Worldly-minded" rings similar to the apostle John's reminder against the lust of the flesh and the eyes, and the boastful pride of life. These are not from the Father but from the world that is passing away (1 John 2:16-17). "Devoid of the Spirit" proves that these men were not born again. They had never received the Holy Spirit or Christ as their personal Savior. Only believers, who have the Spirit, are able to call God, Father (Gal. 4:6). Kistemaker writes that these men

> claimed to have the Spirit and to be morally free in respect to their behavior. Most likely they indicated that the Christians lacked this gift. Jude, however, turns the matter around and states that the heretics "follow mere natural instincts and do not have the Spirit." These people are apostates. In a few words Jude has put the godless men in their place. They have no part in the church, for they lack the Spirit of God.[3]

Manton adds that "devoid of the Spirit"

> is added not only to show that they were destitute of true grace and regeneration, but partly to rebuke their vain pretences. The Gnostics and other filthy seducers of that time did arrogate to themselves a singularity and peculiarity of the Spirit, as if all others were carnal, and they only had the Spirit; whereas indeed the contrary was true, they, giving up themselves to such filthy practices, showed that they had nothing of the Spirit in them.[4]

Verse 20 begins as did verse 17—"But you." The contrast of the readers and the accused false teachers is striking. Several things are given as means to mature the readers in the apostolic faith and to counter the false teaching of the apostates (vv. 20–23). Specific responsibilities are given to "the called, beloved in God the Father, and kept for Jesus Christ" (v. 1) in these verses. Jude simply calls them "beloved" here (v. 20).

God's written revelation is the means by which the readers could build themselves up "on your most holy faith" (v. 20; cf. v. 3). The divine deposit of truth is in view. It is "most holy," setting it apart from all other messages. "Praying in the Holy Spirit" (v. 20) is another means by which the false teachers are to be approached (see 2 Cor. 10:3–5).

To be "building yourselves up" is an act of moral and spiritual responsibility. There is a proper spiritual and proper exertion in doing this. However, this cannot be taken as "a self-work." Self-effort in the spiritual realm will fail. All believers are dependent upon the work of the Lord in the Christian endeavor of growing in grace. In the *most holy faith* refers to the Christian life that is founded on trust. Believers should seek to establish themselves firmly in the great doctrines, and in the practice of what is one's duty as a child of God. Placing one's self on the permanent foundation of faith is the opposite of what some do—separate themselves from believers and from the truth. Those who depart from biblical truth are conceited. To have trust in one's own foundation should be the same as having faith in the foundation of Christ. *Most holy faith* is presented by Jude as the opposite to the most unholy quicksand of the doctrines condemned in the New Testament.

Three participles in Jude 1:20–21 spell out what is necessary to keep oneself in the love of God and thus able to withstand the false teaching. The three participles are building, praying, and waiting (vv. 20–21).[5]

Ellicott notes that only *praying in the Holy Spirit* "can Christians make firm their foundation. The Greek admits of [in the Holy Spirit] being taken with the previous clause. . . . It means that we pray in His strength and wisdom: He moves our hearts and directs our petitions. (See Rom. 8:26)."[6]

When the readers are urged to *keep yourselves in the love of God*, Jude is thinking of

> the love of God for the readers and not their love for God. To keep oneself in God's love is to stay where God can love us as his children and can shower upon us all the gifts of love that he has for those who are his children.

The final participle states what is to accompany this keeping of themselves in God's love: "expecting the mercy of our Lord Jesus Christ for eternal life," expecting it in unwavering hope. It is the mercy that Christ will grant us at the last day, in the final judgment.[7]

The recipients of Jude's letter must not only stand firm in their faith and defend it; they must also seek to salvage others entrapped in false teaching. They were saved to serve as are all of God's children. Those who were doubting were to be shown mercy (v. 22).

> It seems certain that this verse is talking about believers in Christ who have a shaky faith, i.e., they are being influenced by the false prophets who are sowing confusion. They are not in danger of losing their salvation but they are in danger of spiritual shipwreck. They need to be restored to sound trust in the Lord, and in what they believe about biblical doctrine. Who *are doubting* here in what is called the middle voice means *to have misgivings, in confusion making wrong distinctions*, or *to be drawn into quarrelsome interpretations and explanations*. Often, it has the force of being led into *disputes over opinions.*[8]

They needed understanding and help from those stronger in the faith. Some, it appears, were already in the fire, which describes the false teaching. These, Jude writes, need a more direct and frontal approach. They need to be snatched quickly from the error of their way (cf. Zech. 3:2). Both groups are to be extended mercy—those doubting (v. 22) and those already engrossed in the error (v. 23).

Doubting disputers are really in great spiritual danger. They need to be corrected and convinced that they are going in the wrong direction. Jude uses what is called an iterative (addressing a problem) present imperative that builds with certain intensity. "Save others, snatching them out of the fire" by using heroic measures and quick action. Jude seems to be quoting Amos 4:11 that reads, "As a firebrand plucked out of the burning," or Zechariah 3:2 that says, "A brand plucked out of the burning." The apostle does not address how this is to be accomplished. It might be assumed that any legitimate means can be applied. Yet, it is possible that some have gone too far. Some may have gone too far and no amount of pleading will do any good. Often pity is all that is left to give. "In fear" explains somewhat the "hating even the garment polluted by the flesh." Some think Jude is saying something like, "Lest by our pity for them we ourselves become spotted." ("Spotted" in the Greek is *spiloō* and may refer to excrement on the garments.) Others believe Jude is writing about wayward believers who return to the fellowship, and that the mercifully receiving them is to be carried out "with fear." "But, surely, those that are still spotted with filth cannot be received back to be handled with fear, gingerly, at arm's length, lest we get this filth also on ourselves. The participle (of *spiloō*) is [in] the perfect tense, which means that the spots and the stains of the past are still present. People of this kind, who are wearing such a tunic, surely cannot be taken back; they must first be thoroughly cleaned by repentance."[9]

Jude here is giving a very visual and expressive illustration. The *filth* or *pollution* is graphic, and by using this word, Jude seems to be warning those to whom he is writing to avoid such a condition. Though believers may go to great lengths to save such, great caution must be taken to avoid going with them in their sins. Those so trapped must be seen as practicing loathsome and contagious transgressions. One must take precaution to maintain moral purity. There is much wisdom in the warnings of Jude. While trying to save the sinner, we must still detest his sins. "Not a few have been deeply corrupted in their attempts to reform the polluted. There never could be, for example, too much circumspection and prayer for personal safety from pollution."[10]

Contemporary culture is becoming indifferent to the question of truth. Christians have found truth in Jesus (Eph 4:21). Jude warns of the dangers in the mixture of error with this truth. So his eloquent tract for maintaining the purity and truth of the Christian faith is needed in view of the relativity and syncretism so common today. While it must be granted that some Christians have been and are still intolerantly dogmatic about relatively minor theological issues, there is also the great danger of accepting uncritically all teaching or positions as valid and thus compromising God's once-and-for-all self-disclosure in Jesus.[11]

Encouragement (Jude 1:24–25)

Jude's readers were faced with terrible danger from false teachers. They were no doubt fearful and frustrated. His closing word to them must have come as a great source of comfort and encouragement. These verses contain one of the great doxologies of the New Testament.

God the Father is the one who keeps His own from falling. With "who is able" Jude uses the present participle of *dunamai*. God has the power and authority, on an ongoing basis, to keep His children from stumbling. He is continually capable of holding the believer up. By using the participle, Jude is saying in so many words, that it is God's very nature and character to do this for the saints. "To keep you from stumbling" may be better translated "to keep you unfallen." With Jude's strong, severe, and sober warnings, pronouncements, and exhortations, here he changes his tone to joy and encouragement. "To keep you" means "to guard you." The Lord is vitally concerned and active in aiding His own. The preservation of the Christian was mentioned at the beginning of the letter in verse 1, "there it was because of their relation with Christ; here it is divine power that will keep. A marked feature of the true saint is his sense of weakness, he is a complete contrast to the haughty independent and presumptuous impostors. His strength is in God, who can so preserve him that he will not even stumple."[12]

It is clearly a hazard to live the Christian walk in a climate of heresy and false teachers. In time, this will affect the morals of the believer and compromise will set in. As already mentioned, it can even be dangerous to witness in a filthy moral environment because of the danger from being polluted by temptations that are so strong. If one gets too close to the fire, one is burned! The child of God must ask if he is strong in the Lord's might and protection.

This doxology of these last two verses recalls the power of God. Like Jude here, Paul was often driven to his knees because of the glory ascribed to the Lord (Rom. 16:25; Eph. 3:20). Jude ends this letter with similar heartfelt adoration. This is why believers must keep themselves "in the love of God" as he mentioned in verse 21. "From stumbling" is *aptaistous* with the more dramatic idea of kept "from falling." This word is only used here in the New Testament but in Classical Greek Xenophon used it to describe a horse that does not stumble because he is surefooted. Plutarch uses the word to speak of the steady falling of snow. And Epictetus uses the word to picture a man who does not fall and have moral lapses.[13]

> This doxology is truly magnificent in its conception and scope. It probably owes something to traditional liturgical material which was circulating even as early as the fifties of the first century: see the close parallels in Ephesians 1:4; 5:27; Colossians 1:22; 1 Thessalonians 3:13. But the picture sketched is Jude's own. It seems the faithful Christians among his readers, after all the pressures of contending for the faith in a licentious age and permissive church, standing before God like perfect sacrifices in his heavenly sanctuary, in self-offering to the glory of God amidst the joyous jubilation of the redeemed.[14]

Simon Kistemaker aptly concludes:

> Jude writes a letter to strengthen the readers in their faith and to warn them not to be misled by apostates who in life and doctrine try to lead them astray. After identifying himself, he greets the recipients and pronounces a blessing of mercy, peace, and love. Jude reminds the believers of three Old Testament examples that illustrate divine judgment: the unbelieving Israelites in the desert, the rebellious angels who left their positions of authority, and the immoral men of Sodom and Gomorrah. The readers know about the coming of the scoffers, for the apostles have

given them instructions. Jude urges the believers to strengthen one another in the faith and to wait prayerfully for the realization of eternal life. He exhorts them to show mercy to doubters, to save others from destruction, and to be wary of sin's contamination. He concludes his epistle with a splendid doxology to God.[15]

Jude reminds his readers that the Lord of the Old Testament is the "only" God. Gnosticism would have been eroding that truth and some may have been infected with the disease of doubt! Throughout the New Testament the Lord Jesus is amply designated as the Savior, but in verse 25 Jude reminds us that God is also known as the Savior (Ps. 106:21; Isa. 43:11; 45:15; Hosea 13:4; 1 Tim. 1:1; 2:3; Titus 2:13). But it is only "through Jesus Christ our Lord" that we can recognize Him as such, and give to Him the right praise to His glory. Some scholars have well noted that Jude places *through Jesus Christ our Lord* in close proximity to the fact that God is also our Savior. In the construction, the two ideas are united.

Jude ascribes four important descriptions to God the Father in the close of his letter. Again, this could have been done on purpose to counter the weak view of deity taught by the Gnostics. *Glory* ("*doxa*") conjures up the idea of the brilliant splendor and perfect radiance of the Lord. The word touches on the holiness of God in that there is no sin or imperfection to spoil His very essence. "Majesty" (*megalosune*) refers to His "eminence, majesty," and is related to the word *megas* describing the Father's "greatness, significance." "Dominion" (*kratos*) points to His "power, sovereignty," and even His *great intensity* of Person. In other words, there is no other being as powerful as our God! "Authority" (*exousia*) is a common but important word that reminds us of His "unlimited ability, freedom to act." On the way this word is so often used, Balz and Schneider write:

> There is no appeal to a higher norm against God's authority. Thus his right and creative freedom are compared with the power of a potter who can form from clay whatever he wishes (Rom. 9:21). This divine perfect power is not only affirmed in argument, but is also confessed doxologically (Jude 25). However, God allows his Son to participate in his authority, and has given to him the power to exercise judgment (John 5:27).[16]

If God were but a stranger to us, He would still be worthy of such an acknowledgment as found in this doxology. However, when considering who He truly is, and what He has so graciously done for us, it is difficult to hold back such expressions of honor. And this is what must have deeply touched the emotions of Jude as he penned these final words. The heart must ponder and be exercised until it is filled with the knowledge of His great benefits and love. Then the spirit of the Christian cannot remain quiet. It must break forth into such praise. A gracious heart must have a sense of God's worth and perfection, that it must ascribe all honor and glory to His nature. "When we have done our utmost we come short; . . . Yet it is good to do as much as we can. Love to God will not be satisfied with a little praise. . . . Love enlarges the heart towards God."[17]

At the very close of verse 25, Jude writes, "before all time and now and forever. Amen." This better reads, *before all the eon, and now, and for all the eons.* Lenski rightly notes:

> "Before all the eons" means in all eternity, before the whole world eons of time began; "for all the eons" means for all eternity (which is conceived as eons upon eons). Between them is "now," language which sectionalizes eternity, which is the opposite of time and cannot be divided even in thought. Scripture condescends to our mental limitation.[18]

God's power and love are assured. They must discharge their responsibilities just spelled out. But those by themselves would be of no avail without the awesome power and purpose of God. To Him, therefore, belongs all the "glory, majesty, dominion and authority, before all time and now and forever" (v. 25).

Study Questions

1. How does Jude specifically encourage his readers?

2. List all the ways Jude describes the false teachers.

3. What does it mean to pray in the Holy Spirit?

4. Are verses 22 and 23 speaking of the saved or the unsaved?

The Antichrist

Biblical Teaching on the Antichrist

Though John mentions "antichrist" only five times, and then only in his epistles (1 John 2:18 (2), 22; 4:3, 2 John 1:7), a more complete teaching on the subject ranges throughout both the Old and New Testaments, probably beginning in Genesis 3:15.

In John's first epistle, he also writes about the *principle* of antichrist and about those who become antichrists in their religious lies, with which they maliciously deceive others, leading them astray.

To completely comprehend the personality and the works of the Antichrist, one must understand him within the framework of a counterfeit trinity. Revelation 13:1–18 teaches that an unholy tri-unity will come about with Satan acting out the role of God the Father. As the Lord gave His authority to the Son, Satan will grant all power to the Antichrist. To a degree, the False Prophet is the counterfeit Holy Spirit and urges people to worship the Antichrist, or the Beast.

The Title or Descriptions of the Antichrist

Many passages, such as Revelation 13, show the Antichrist's extensive activities. Below are the main titles ascribed to him.

Seed of Satan. Though not all scholars agree, Genesis 3:15 could be an ancient and cryptic reference to this evil personality who is "birthed" by Satan himself, as portrayed by the serpent in this passage. With the disobedience of Adam and Eve (Gen. 3:1–7), the devil played a vital role in the temptation of our early parents. Genesis 3:15 gives the prophetic judgment against Satan, though the words are directed toward the serpent: "And I will put enmity between you [Satan embodying the serpent] and the woman [Eve], and between your seed [possibly the Antichrist] and her seed [the Messiah]; he shall bruise you on the head, and you shall bruise him on the heel." As seen by both pious Jewish and Christian commentators, this is an utterance of the unfolding historic struggle between the promised Messiah and the evil activities of Satan.

The Little Horn. This evil personality surfaces in one of the most graphic prophecies of Daniel the seer of the Lord (Daniel 7). Daniel describes "ten horns" (vv. 7–8) that will comprise the final form of the last great world power, Rome. He then envisions "another horn," "a little one" (v. 8) that has superhuman and near-supernatural powers, and who is then able to speak great boastings. He is further described as "the other horn" (v. 20) and the one who "will speak out against the Most High and wear down the saints of the Highest One" (v. 25).

The Prince. Daniel describes him in 9:26–27 as "the prince" whose people will come and destroy the city of Jerusalem in A.D. 70. The applicable part of the passage reads: "the people of the prince who is to come will destroy the city and the sanctuary. . . . And he will make a firm covenant with the many for one week [heptad, referring to a seven-year period], but in the middle of the week he will put a stop to sacrifice. . . ."

The revised Roman Empire will be the last great government during end-time events. Rome also was the nation in its earliest form that occupied the Holy Land and was responsible for destroying the temple and the city of Jerusalem. The prince, or Antichrist, will arise from its new form in the future. The covenant he will make will probably be a seven-year peace pact with the Jews who will be restored to the Holy Land. In the middle of that seven-year period, he will break the covenant and stop the sacrifice practiced in the rebuilt sanctuary.

Though these verses are somewhat complicated, most Bible scholars admit they refer to this future personality called the Antichrist. Harry Bultema writes that the verses here begin with the destruction of the city of Jerusalem in A.D. 70, some thirty years or so after the execution of the Jesus the Messiah. He adds, "All orthodox exegetes agree on this." Bultema then shows that the same exegetes who hold this view follow the proper rules of prophetic writings. "So in Daniel and Revelation the Antichrist is considered the head and embodiment of the fourth and final world power. . . . He will set himself up in the temple and pretend to be God (see Dan. 11:36 and 2 Thess. 2:4)."[1]

One Who Makes Desolate. This phrase is found in the context that continues from Daniel 9:26. Verse 27 reads: " . . . will come one who makes desolate, even until a complete destruction, . . . " The work of the Antichrist in destroying the temple that stands in this final seven-year period will bring about a downward spiral hastening the terrible final months of this time period known as the Tribulation. Jesus said that if this period does not end, by the Lord's dramatic intervention, "no life would [be] saved" (Matt. 24:22). The Antichrist brings on the ultimate chaotic moment for all of human history!

The King [Who] Will Do As He Pleases. While almost all Bible commentators believe the great historic tyrant Antiochus Epiphanes (175–164 B.C.) is without doubt prophetically described in Daniel 11:21–35, they believe the Antichrist himself is portrayed in verses 36–45. He magnifies himself, speaks monstrous things against God, and will apparently prosper until "that which is decreed will be done" (v. 36). When his end comes at the end of the seven-year Tribulation period, "no one will help him" (v. 45).

The Man of Lawlessness. In 2 Thessalonians 2 the apostle Paul gives three descriptions of the Antichrist. Paul in verse 3 describes him as "the man of lawlessness" who will be revealed. In 2:8 the apostle simply calls him "the lawlessness one." *Lawlessness* comes from *anomias,* meaning that he is above law, or without law. "He will be a law unto himself, making his own laws and despising the laws of God. This is a man and not [simply] a religion or religious system."[2]

The Son of Destruction. In 2 Thessalonians 2:3 "destruction" is *apolia* and means "perdition," that is, "the son who is due destruction and punishment," which describes his just end. "Judas was called by Christ the son of destruction (John 17:12), and Peter, more than any other writer, uses the word in regard to a future judgment (2 Peter 2:1, 2, 3; 3:7, 16). It is sometimes translated 'damnation' (2:3)."[3]

As Being God. Paul writes in 2 Thessalonians 2:4 that the Antichrist someday "takes his seat in the temple of God, displaying himself as being God." Here the Antichrist is taking the very name of deity. His boldness is not blunted at this halfway period in the seven-year Tribulation. In this verse "the apostle is describing the Antichrist's desecration of the temple, something that [in the future] must follow the apostasy. His blasphemy manifests itself in his 'displaying himself as being God.'"[4]

Antichrist Is Coming. For the first time in the biblical accounts, this evil person is called *Antichrist* by the apostle John. "Children, it is the last hour; and just as you heard that antichrist is coming, even now many antichrists have arisen" (1 John 2:18). John's use of the word seems to follow logically his warnings in the previous verses (vv. 16–17) about the evil world that is in the process of passing away. The world system is in opposition to God as the antichrist will be also.

The Conquering One Riding a White Horse. When the Tribulation is opened with the seal judgments (Rev. 6:1–17), one rides forth who has a bow and a crown (v. 2). He goes out "conquering, and to conquer." Because he is on a white horse, some believe he is the Lord Jesus coming to do battle against sin. Though it is true that at the end of the Tribulation, at the second coming of Christ, Jesus the Messiah indeed will come riding a white horse of justice and victory (19:11), it is likely that the Tribulation begins with the Antichrist appearing like a conquering savior and hero to unsuspecting humanity.

Some have said the first rider in Revelation 6 will be Christ at His second coming, because the white horse is a symbol of victory. This view, however, seems unlikely, because Christ the Lamb had just broken the seal. And it would seem strange to have Christ depicted in this way at the beginning of the Tribulation, when He will come on a white horse after the Tribulation is over, not at its beginning. The rider then will be "the prince who is to come" (Dan. 9:26), the false messiah or the Antichrist, as revealed in Revelation 13:1–10.[5]

The Beast That Comes Out of the Abyss. From Revelation 11:7 on throughout the Apocalypse, John made the Antichrist one of his most important themes. An entire book could be written as to how he is portrayed in 13:1–10 and in many other verses that follow. His final demise is graphically described in 19:20: "And the beast was seized, and . . . thrown alive into the lake of fire which burns with brimstone."

The Rabbinical Description of the Antichrist

The ancient Jewish rabbis describe the person and work of the antichrist with remarkable detail.[6] Although this is virtually an unknown fact to most Christian students of the Scriptures, it is true. The rabbis understood the significance of the prophetic utterances about this evil character the Jews called Armilus.

Patai writes, "Remarkable is the statement in one version of the Midrash [commentary] that he is called 'Antichrist.'" The rabbis believe he was first mentioned in the messianic prophecy of Isaiah 11:1–4, where it is said that the Shoot, the Son of David who comes forth from David's father Jesse, is the One who slays with "the breath of His lips" the wicked one, or Antichrist.

The origin of the word *Armilus* is of some foreign influence. Some see the origin from the historic Roman personage Romulus, from Heremolaos, i.e., "Destroyer of peoples." From the Midrash *Aseret haSh'vatim*, it is said that Satan will descend to Rome and issue a decree against the Jewish people. The

Messiah, the Son of David, will then come and rescue Israel. And they will all dwell in safety all His days.

Sometimes the rabbis interpreted Rome as Edom, to which the Antichrist will go and say, "I am your Messiah, I am your god!" He will mislead many who will follow him and believe he is their king. But Michael, the Great Prince, will blow the shofar to signal the arrival of the forerunner Elijah and the Messiah. Elijah will cry out, "This is the Messiah!" When the Messiah ben David comes, "he will kill the wicked Armilus. . . . And thereafter the Holy One, blessed be He, will gather Israel who are dispersed here and there."[7]

Evidence indicates that the Jewish scholars of old put together this portrait of the Antichrist from both Old and New Testament references.

Will the Antichrist Be a Jew or a Gentile?

Some believe that the Antichrist will be Jewish. Their argument is based on the fact that the Jewish people in the Tribulation accept him as the Messiah, and they would only do this if they thought he was Jewish. The other position holds that more than likely the Antichrist is a Gentile of Roman or European origins.

The debate on this questions has its roots in Daniel 11:37 which describes the dastardly behavior of the future Antichrist when he will assume worldwide power. In the previous verse Daniel predicts that the Antichrist will be "the king [who] will do as he pleases, and he will exalt and magnify himself above every god, and will speak monstrous things against the God of gods." The disputed verse 37 then follows: "And he will show no regard for the gods of his fathers. . . ."

The Hebrew word *elohim*, though a plural word, should be translated "god" when referring to pagan deities. But the same plural word is used when identifying the Lord God of the Old Testament. Most evangelical scholars attest that the plural form opens the door for the later developed doctrine of the Trinity and the plurality of the persons in the Godhead.

The King James Version brought on part of the problem when the translators ignored the larger context of the verses and translated verse 37 as "The God of his fathers."

The Antichrist Is Jewish

On this position, Arnold Fruchtenbaum writes:

> The whole argument rests on the phrase "the God of his fathers" which is taken to be clear-cut evidence that the Antichrist is a Jew. It should be

pointed out, however, that the argument for the Jewishness of the Antichrist from this verse is based upon the King James Version.

Ultimately, Bible doctrine should be based on the Hebrew and Greek texts since they are the closest to the original autographs. . . . Any student of Hebrew would see from the original text that the correct translation should be: "the *gods* of his fathers," and not "the *God* of his fathers." In the whole context, Daniel 11:36–39, the term *god* is used a total of eight times. In the Hebrew text, six of these times it is in the singular and twice in the plural, one of which is the phrase in verse 37. The very fact that the plural form of the word "god" is used in a context where the singular is found in the majority of cases makes this a reference to heathen deities and not a reference to the God of Israel. . . . The earliest known translation of the Old Testament is the Septuagint (LXX), which is a Greek translation of the Old Testament made about 250 B.C. The LXX has translated the word as "gods" which is in keeping with the Hebrew text. . . . Furthermore, the New Scofield Reference Bible, itself based on the King James Version, has done a great service to scholarship by rendering this passage to read in the plural form.[8]

The Antichrist Is a Gentile

More compelling are the arguments that show the Antichrist will come forth at the beginning of the Tribulation from the nations, especially from the revived Roman Empire. At least four biblical arguments tell us the antichrist is a Gentile: (1) his identification with future Rome; (2) biblical typology and Antiochus Epiphanes; (3) The nature of the times of the Gentiles; and (4) the biblical imagery that he comes out of the sea, or the Gentile nations.

1. Daniel makes two important references to the "Prince," or Antichrist, in his prophecy 9:24–27. He tells us that "the people of the prince" come and destroy the city (Jerusalem) and the sanctuary (the temple) at some future time. Almost all scholars agree this took place in A.D. 70. Few historians deny that "the people" are the Romans, who are occupying Jerusalem. The prince then comes out of the revived Roman Empire that is in place during the Tribulation.

2. Just before Daniel makes reference to the Antichrist, "the king" in Daniel 11:36–45, he describes the perfect type of the Antichrist, the Gentile Antiochus Epiphanes IV (175–164 B.C.), in verses 21–35. Fruchtenbaum adds: "Nowhere is a Gentile seen as a type of Christ; and with good reason, for Christ Himself was a Jew. So here, the type of the Antichrist is a Gentile, Antiochus Epiphanes. The reason is that the Antichrist himself is to be a Gentile."[9]

3. Most premillennialists agree that the "times of the Gentiles" mentioned in Luke 21:24 do not end until the second coming of Christ. "It is further agreed that the Antichrist is the final ruler of the times of the Gentiles."[10]

4. In John's lengthy description of the activity of the Antichrist in Revelation 13:1–10, the apostle envisions him "coming up out of the sea" (v. 1). This "beast," as John describes him, is carrying on his shoulders the nations that constitute the final form of the Roman Empire. They are the "ten horns and seven heads" described in Daniel 7:20–24.

All of these arguments together would tell us that the Antichrist is more than likely a charismatic and powerful Gentile world leader who is able to unite and manipulate for a time the great nations of the earth.

APPENDIX 2

The Doctrine of Confession

The word "confess" comes from two Greek words (*homo* = *like; logos* = *word*). "Confession" then is *like-wording*, or calling something as it really is. Especially when referring to sin, confession means that we describe that sin as God describes it!

Confession *("homologeo")* can be, in some situations, almost equal to having faith, or believing. For example, in John 9:22 we read, "For the Jews had already agreed, that if anyone should *confess* [Jesus] to be Christ, he should be put out of the synagogue." However, in another instance, the apostle John separates confession from faith when he writes about the rules of the Pharisees: "Nevertheless many even of the rulers *believed* in [Jesus], but because of the Pharisees they were not *confessing* Him, lest they should be put out of the synagogue" (12:42, emphasis mine). Here John is saying that some of the rulers certainly believed in the Lord but were not *outwardly expressing* that belief.

At first glance, in Romans 10:8–11 it may seem that Paul is contradicting what John wrote in his gospel. Paul says in verses 9–10, "If you confess with your mouth Jesus as Lord, and believe in your heart that God raised Him from the dead, you shall be saved; for with the heart man believes, resulting in righteousness, and with the mouth he confesses, resulting in salvation." Does Paul here mean that there is no salvation without confession? Not really.

Notice that Paul reverses the order in the two verses. In verse 9 he says *confess* and *believe*, then he changes the order and writes *believes* and *confesses*. He bookends this discussion in verses 8 and 11. In verse 8 he quotes Deuteronomy 30:14, which says, "The word is very near you, in your mouth and in your heart"—that is, what one truly believes in the heart is right there in front, about to come out of the mouth!

If Paul were truly adamant that salvation must come through confession, he would not have closed his discussion in Romans by quoting Isaiah 28:16 in 10:11: "For the Scripture says, 'Whoever believes in Him will not be disappointed.'" The outcome of belief and faith will be confession with the mouth!

The New Testament also uses *confession* in the sense of giving a testimony. Paul writes to Timothy, "You made the good confession in the presence of many witnesses" (1 Tim. 6:12). The word is also used in the negative sense to describe those who give a shallow and meaningless confession. Paul further writes about those deniers who run away from the truth, who "profess [*"confess"*] to know God, but by their deeds they deny Him" (Titus 1:16).

To maintain fellowship with the Lord and with other believers requires the confession of our sins (1 John 1:9); otherwise, we live as hypocrites who fail to admit that as children of God we can sin and damage relationships.

Confessing that Jesus came in the flesh is also to John a sign of orthodoxy (1 John 4:2), and those who cannot do so are not from God (v. 3). The apostle adds importance to the issue of confession when he writes, "Whoever confesses that Jesus is the Son of God, God abides in him, and he in God" (v. 15). To counter the growing Gnosticism of his day, John also says, "Those who do not acknowledge [*"confess"*] Jesus Christ as coming in the flesh" are deceivers and like the Antichrist (2 John 7).

To not confess is to deny (1 John 2:23), and to deny is to lie. In the contexts of John's epistles, to deny is to cover the truth that Jesus came in flesh, to hide "the fact that in Jesus Christ we have the eternal Son of God, born of the Virgin, whose blood (1 John 1:7) is the expiation for the sins of the world (1 John 2:2; 4:9, 10), and that 'this One is the real God and life eternal' (1 John 5:20)."[1]

John's Epistles and the Cult of Gnosticism

As the New Testament was being completed, a pagan cult was growing more and more popular in the Mediterranean world. Gnosticism was a multifaceted religion that was adaptable to almost any belief, ethnic group, or philosophy. Many centuries later we still do not know all that was taught in its secret meetings. However, most Bible teachers acknowledge that the apostle John, near the end of his life, was addressing in his epistles some of the Gnostic dangers he saw coming into the churches. Only in a few other places in our New Testament books do we see evidence that the authors may have had this heathen cult in mind when they wrote.

What does the word Gnosticism mean? Gnosticism (or Gnostic) comes from the Greek word *ginōskō,* which means "to know, understand." Our English word *knowledge* comes from the related word *gnosis.* The Gnostics believed they were given a higher spiritual understanding that was far beyond simple faith. They held that the material world was sinful, and therefore Christ could not have come from God and have been born in natural, impure flesh.

Where did Gnosticism come from? This is a difficult question to answer, but most Bible scholars believe that it is a very old belief that certainly was pre-Christian. Some say it had its early roots in ancient Hinduism or in Persian religions. Strong evidence indicates that there were vestiges of it in the Dead Sea Scrolls found at Qumran in 1946 and in Gnostic documents catalogued in the Nag Hammadi library discovered in 1945. Without a doubt, it grew quickly during early New Testament times, and this is why John, writing his epistles late in life, felt compelled to address its dangers.

How did Gnosticism fit into Greek thinking? The most pervasive view is that Gnosticism crossed the line into Christianity by means of certain Greek attitudes. Many Greeks and Romans who were attracted to Christianity felt it needed radical "adjustments" by Gnostic thinking. Historically this has been called "the radical Hellenizing of Christianity." "In this view, Gnosticism resulted from the attempt of early [Greek] Christian thinkers to make Christianity understandable, acceptable, and respectable in a world almost totally permeated by Greek assumptions about the reality of the World."[1]

What Did Gnosticism Teach?

- The God of creation was separate from the God of redemption.
- Christianity was divided into categories with some groups being more superior to others.
- Knowledge was exalted over faith.
- Matter was seen as inferior, sin causing.
- Some Gnostics such as Marcion rejected the Old Testament, feeling it was more materialistic than the New, being based on law rather than grace.
- Even if Christ were God, He would not enter into the incarnate state, since flesh is sinful.
- Christ only seemed to appear to be a person; He was not.
- "Spiritual" Christians lived on a higher plain than ordinary Christians.
- "Secret" knowledge was stressed.
- Secret, rather than intellectual knowledge, was given by Jesus Himself.
- Knowledge of salvation came by ritual, or secret, instruction.
- Ultimately, salvation came by self-discovery.

In their Gospel accounts, both Luke and John may be emphasizing the reality of Christ's bodily resurrection in order to answer Gnostic thinking. Luke tells how the Lord spoke with some of the disciples along the Emmaus road following His resurrection. As they shared their experience with the other disciples, Jesus appeared in their midst, and they thought they were seeing a "spirit" (Luke 24:37). But Jesus said to them, "Touch Me and see, for a spirit does not have flesh and bones as you see that I have" (v. 39).

When told that Jesus had come out of the grave, Thomas said, "Unless I shall see in His hands the imprint of the nails, and put my finger into the place of the nails, and put my hand into His side, I will not believe" (John 20:25). But after touching the Lord, the reality of the resurrected body brought forth the cry, "My Lord and my God!" (v. 28).

These two historic accounts would go to the heart of Gnostic belief, proving that Jesus was not simply a spirit apparition but the resurrected Son of God.

How does John answer the Gnostics? In more than twelve verses John seems to address his concerns about the Gnostic heresy.

John begins by noting that we do not fully understand what our new resurrected and eternal flesh will be like, but it will be a *real* body like the body of Christ. In fact, "we shall be like Him, because we shall see Him just as He is" (1 John 3:2). This counters the Gnostic position that flesh, even resurrected flesh, is evil.

John warns of false spirits that teach Jesus did not come in the flesh or from God the Father (1 John 4:2–3). Those who deny this reality about the person of Christ "speak as from the world, and the world listens to them" (v. 5). Those who teach such lies are false prophets (v. 1). Those who do not listen to these deceptive lies "know the Spirit of God" (v. 2).

John continues to answer Gnostic thinking by reminding his readers that God's love is manifested in them, because they understand that God "has sent His only begotten Son into the world so that we might live through Him" (v. 9). By saying this, John answers the Gnostic view that there is more than one true God and that Christ is not deity. John again addresses this issue in verse 15: "Whoever confesses that Jesus is the Son of God, God abides in him, and he in God."

John's Use of *Kosmos*

In most references to *kosmos* the New Testament writers have in mind the evil world system or the philosophy of a sinful mind-set that runs counter to spiritual truth. John uses *kosmos* far more than any other writer—106 times, whereas Paul uses the word only about 48 times in all of his epistles. All the New Testament writers, and the Lord Jesus, use the word generally the same way. Only a few times does it refer to the earth itself. One such example is when Christ told His disciples that soon "He should depart out of this world to the Father" (John 13:1). The word may also refer to all the inhabitants of earth as a collective group of human beings, the *kosmos*.

Some Ways John Uses Kosmos in His Epistles

- *Jesus is the propitiation ("the mercy seat," "the place of satisfaction") for "the whole world" (1 John 2:2).*
- *Christians are not to love what the world considers most important. "Do not love the world, nor the things in the world" (1 John 2:15).*
- *The lusts and boastful pride of the world are not from the Father (1 John 2:16).*
- *The world and all it holds dear is temporary. "The world is passing away" (1 John 2:17).*
- *The world hates believers (1 John 3:13).*
- *Materialism, or "the world's goods," make believers selfish, and they cannot see their brothers' and sisters' needs (1 John 3:17).*
- *False prophets can deceive the people of the world (1 John 4:1).*
- *God sent His Son into the world in order to save sinners (1 John 4:9).*
- *Jesus is the Savior of the people of the world (1 John 4:14).*
- *Overcoming the sinful spiritual pull of the world, through believing in Christ, brings about salvation. The overcomer "believes that Jesus is the Son of God" (1 John 5:5).*
- *"The whole world lies in the power of the evil one (Satan)" (1 John 5:19).*

Teaching through First John

First John is a family epistle. In it are found truths especially and exclusively for the children of God. Your heart will be thrilled as you study and preach from this book penned by one who was very close to the Lord. In John's day many were denying and rejecting the faith. This epistle is a defense of the person of Christ in a very real sense, yet it also marks out the path believers must walk if they are to enjoy fellowship with God and other believers. The standards and rules of conduct set forth in this epistle serve as a means of determining our relationship with the Lord. John delineates certain things that will be true and certain things that will not be true of the child of God.

At first glance the book may appear very simple and easy to understand, yet the very nature of the book makes it difficult to understand in spots. Because Paul wrote with lawyer-like logic as he presented his case, his letters are much easier to follow than John's. John writes more like a musician. He develops a general primary theme throughout his first epistle and brings in many secondary themes that relate to and are dependent on the main theme. These secondary themes are not developed fully; thus many questions concerning them are left unanswered and we must go elsewhere in Scripture for more teaching on these subjects.

This means that much study is required to master this book. The first and basic preparation is to read through the entire epistle at one sitting before preaching from it.[1]

Do not forget as you teach from 1 John, or any other book or text for that matter, that we all need to do our homework and immerse ourselves in prayer as we prepare. The honor and duty of the person in the pulpit is to preach the whole counsel of God in the power of the Holy Spirit. It is not the preacher's responsibility to bring conviction; that is the work of the Spirit of God. Speak the truth in love (Eph. 4:15). That is not easy. Neither truth nor love is hard to set forth separately, but proclaiming the two together harmoniously is God's call to the man of God.

It is always good to give proper attention to the background of the author and the book before teaching through it. As you go through the book, be looking for ways to relate truth to the author's purpose for writing the book.

Each of the major sections (I, II, etc.) of the outline below constitutes plenty of material for one lesson. As you prepare and teach through 1 John, look for ways to emphasize truths that your people especially need. Also, look for illustrations from contemporary issues to illustrate truths.

Spend sufficient time preparing your introductions and conclusions. These are very important. Get the people's attention and then give them an impression of your main emphasis at the end.

Following is a detailed outline for teaching from 1 John.

I. Overview of 1 John

    A. Background of the Book

        1. Author

        2. Date

        3. People addressed

        4. John's epistle and his gospel

    B. Purposes of the Book

        1. To provide fellowship and joy (1:3-4)

        2. To prevent sin (2:1)

        3. To promote love (2:5-10)

        4. To proclaim forgiveness (2:12)

        5. To prepare believers for opposition (2:26)

        6. To provide a basis for assurance (5:13)

    C. Theme of the Book

        1. The theme stated (1:3)

        2. The theme expanded (1:5; 4:8; 5:20)

II. Fellowship with God (1:1-7)

    A. The Declaration of Fellowship with God (1:1-4)

        1. The humanity of Christ (1:1)

        2. The deity of Christ (1:2)

3. The reason for the declaration (1:3-4)

B. The Description of Fellowship with God (1:5-6)

1. God—the standard (1:5)

2. Sin—the barrier (1:6)

C. The Delight of Fellowship with God (1:7)

1. Walking in the light (1:7a)

2. Fellowship one with another (1:7b)

3. Cleansing from sin (1:7c)

III. Sin and the Child of God (1:8—2:6)

A. The Reality of the Believer's Sin (1:8, 10)

B. The Remedy for the Believer's Sin (1:9; 2:1-2)

C. The Reminder to the Believer (2:3-6)

IV. Fellowship with God and the Believer's Walk (2:7-17)

A. The Commandment (2:7-8)

1. Description of the old (2:7)

2. Description of the new (2:8)

B. The Positive Aspect of the Commandment (2:9-11)

1. Light and love (2:9-10)

2. Darkness and hate (2:11)

C. The Purpose of the Commandment (2:12-14)

1. The persons instructed (2:12-13)

2. The purpose of the instruction (2:12-14)

D. The Negative Aspect of the Commandment (2:15-17)

1. The command stated (2:15)

2. The command defended (2:16-17)

V. Antichrists in the Last Times (2:18-27)

A. The Reality of Antichrists (2:18-19)

1. Their presence (2:18)

2. Their departure (2:19)

B. The Recognition of Antichrists (2:20-23)

1. The believer's acquisition of truth (2:20-21)

2. The antichrists' denial of truth (2:22–23)

C. The Refuge from the teaching of Antichrists (2:24–27)

    1. The assurance of the refuge (2:24–25)

    2. The accomplishment of the refuge (2:26–27)

VI. Fellowship with the Lord and His Return (2:28—3:3)

    A. Preparation for the Lord's Return (2:28)

        1. The positive reason (2:28a)

        2. The negative reason (2:28b)

    B. Occupation in View of the Lord's Return (2:29—3:1)

        1. The believer's righteous acts (2:29)

        2. The Father's love for the believer (3:1a)

        3. The world's hatred of the believer (3:1b)

    C. Transformation at the Lord's return (3:2)

        1. The believer's present position (3:2a)

        2. The believer's future position (3:2b)

    D. Sanctification in view of the Lord's return (3:3)

        1. The people sanctified (3:3a)

        2. The pattern for sanctification (3:3b)

VII. Sins, Satan, the Savior, and the Sons of God (3:4–12)

    A. Sin and the Savior (3:4–5)

        1. The nature of sin (3:4)

        2. The sacrifice of the Savior (3:5)

    B. Sin and the Sons of God (3:6–12)

        1. Evidences of sonship (3:6–7)

        2. Characteristics of sonship (3:8–10)

        3. Manifesting sonship (3:11–12)

VIII. Hate and Love (3:13–24)

    A. Certainty of the World's Hatred (3:13)

    B. Assurance of Eternal Life (3:14–18)

        1. Loving the brethren (3:14–16)

        2. Sharing with the brethren (3:17–18)

C. Assurance in Prayer (3:19–24)

    1. The preparation for prayer (3:19–21)

    2. The practice of prayer (3:22–24)

IX. Beloved, Beware! (4:1–10)

    A. Exhortation to Test the Spirits (4:1–6)

        1. The exhortation (4:1a)

        2. The reason (4:1b)

        3. The test (4:2–3)

        4. The assurance (4:4–6)

    B. Exhortation to Love One Another (4:7–10)

        1. The exhortation (4:7a)

        2. The reason (7b–8)

        3. The example (4:9–10)

X. Union with God and Unity among the Brethren (4:11–21)

    A. Union with God (4:11–19)

        1. God's love (4:11)

        2. God in the believer (4:12)

        3. The believer in God (4:13–16)

        4. Love made perfect (4:17–19)

    B. Unity among the Brethren (4:20–21)

        1. The basis of unity (4:20)

        2. The commandment from God (4:21)

XI. On Being Overcomers (5:1–8)

    A. Basis of the New Birth (5:1a, 6–8)

        1. Personal faith in Christ (5:1a)

        2. The person of Christ (5:6–8)

    B. Evidences of the New Birth (5:1b, 2–3)

        1. Love of the brethren (5:1b)

        2. Obedience to the commandments of God (5:2–3)

    C. Results of the New Birth (5:1c, 4–5)

        1. Membership in God's family (5:1c)

2. Victory over the world (5:4–5)

XII. Wonderful Witness (5:9–15)

A. The Reality of the Witness (5:9)

B. The Recipients of the Witness (5:10–13)

1. Believers contrasted with unbelievers (5:10)

2. Assurance of eternal life (5:13)

C. The Results of Receiving the Witness (John 5:14–15)

1. Heard prayer (5:14)

2. Answered prayer (5:15)

XIII. A Call to Action

A. Counsel Concerning Prayer (5:16–17)

1. Sin not unto death (5:16a, 17)

2. Sin unto death (5:16b)

B. Confession of Certainties (5:18–20)

1. Privileges of divine birth (5:18–19a)

2. Power of the wicked one (5:19b)

3. Preview of divine truth (5:20)

C. Challenge to the Children of God (5:21)

APPENDIX 6

Teaching through Second John

The first thing one must do when preparing to teach John's epistles is to determine the overriding themes. Christian love and God's truth are both stressed in 2 John, yet the primary theme is Christian love.

The following is a suggested outline for 2 John.

Introduction

For the introduction find an illustration of Christian love from some recent endeavor or the total opposite of it from a recent act of violence.

Briefly compare 2 John with 1 and 3 John and Revelation. Be sure to stress that there are three expressions of love in this little book.

I. Responsive Love (2 John 1:1–3)

The "elder" (v. 1) is John the apostle. The "elect lady" (v. 1) is either a woman or a local body of believers, a church. John's loving response to his readers was the result of their response to truth and his own response to the same truth.

II. Obedient Love (2 John 1:4–6)

John rejoiced because of his readers' faithfulness. He urged them to continue to walk or live according to truth, which would be an expression of their love. The readers, and by application all God's people, need to love one another despite differences. Love needs to be displayed, not just defined or declared.

III. Discerning Love (2 John 1:7-11)

Not all who appeared to be followers of Christ were such. Some among the readers were deceivers—antichrists. These were certainly not walking in truth as the believers were exhorted to do. The false teachers among John's readers denied Christ's genuine humanity.

In this section John begins his warning to the faithful in view of the false teachers among them. Those who did not embrace the Christ of Scripture did not have God the Father either. Application can be made here to the many false religions and cults in our time that do not present the Christ of Scripture.

John also gives very serious warning here to those faithful ones to whom he wrote and to us by way of application. For people to allow such a false teacher into their midst and to "give him a greeting" (v. 10) was to "participate in his evil deeds" (v. 11). That is a sobering thought.

Conclusion

1. How may the truths from this short epistle be applied to our lives today?

2. Our love for others should be in response to God and His truth.

3. We too need the reminder to obey God's commands if we really love. In other words, we need to live according to Scripture.

4. Truth matters much. Thus, our love needs to be discerning. Love is not a corrective for false beliefs.

Teaching through Third John

The theme of 3 John seems clearly to be responses to God's truth. The word *truth* appears in verses 1, 3 (two times), 4, 8, and 12 (two times). In each instance the reference is in direct or indirect ways always related to God's truth.

Three persons are named in the book, and each one represents, or is an example of, a specific response to truth. I have outlined the book around these three men.

Introduction

These days there are a lot of examples from public life of not telling the truth. As an attention getter, use a specific instance with which your people are familiar. Or perhaps you would like to refer to Pilate and his perplexed response to Jesus, "What is truth?"

Stress that truth, certainly God's truth, demands a response. This would be a great opportunity to alert your people to the postmodern culture in which we live, where the prevailing view is that there is no absolute truth—everything is relative.

I. Gaius's Response to Truth (3 John 1:1–8)

Gaius, a personal friend of John, responded to truth by walking in it, or living according to it. The result was that Gaius was selfless and received praise from God.

John's and Gaius's lives were garnished with truth. It was the sphere in which their mutual love existed (v. 1). John was deeply and genuinely concerned with Gaius's physical and spiritual well-being. Gaius was very likely a convert of John.

In verses 5 and 6 John begins writing about Gaius's love for God and His people. He helped those in need despite harassment from Diotrephes. This man, Gaius, not only believed, but he also worked, as James said genuine faith would do.

Give special attention to verse 8 and contrast it with 2 John 11. When we help others, we share in the truth they proclaim.

II. Diotrephes' Response to Truth (3 John 1:9–11).

Diotrephes rejected the truth of God, and the result was a life of selfishness and a stern warning from God.

We do not have the letter referred to in verse 9. Diotrephes rejected John's role. Here in contrast to the doctrinal error of rejecting Christ's genuine humanity we have a problem of personal ambition.

John believed in naming sin and dealing with it. Diotrephes' behavior was not only sinful; it was also senseless. In this short book John gives a three-fold moral test for believers. In verses 3 and 4 it is truth, in verse 6 it is love, and in verse 11 it is goodness. John seems to be saying that Diotrephes was not a believer, for his evil deeds indicated he did not know God.

III. Demetrius's Response to Truth (3 John 1:12)

This good man gave testimony to truth, and the result was selflessness and praise from God.

We do not know anything more about this man than we are told here. Maybe he was the carrier of this letter. We do know he was of good report. His testimony was confirmed by truth itself. John agreed fully with the testimonies of others about Demetrius.

Conclusion and Application

Conclude by reviewing briefly how each man responded to truth and what resulted from that.

The last two verses of 3 John were most appropriate for Gaius. He needed to learn to exercise leadership and continue to provide a positive influence among the people in view of the evil work of Diotrephes.

Stress too from the closing of the book the importance of personal greetings. Urge your people to mimic Gaius and Demetrius and avoid the Diotrephes mentality.

The way for each of us to make God's truth prominent in our lives is to exalt Christ, who is Truth, and to humble ourselves before Him.

Conclude, finally, with a reminder to the unsaved that Christ is the Way, the Truth, and the Life, and the only way to heaven.

APPENDIX 8

Teaching through Jude

The theme or major argument of the book of Jude is warning about false teachers.

Jude was a half-brother of the Lord Jesus (Matt. 13:55; Mark 6:3). Apostasy had crept into the early church. Unregenerate people who taught that the more a believer sinned, the more grace was highlighted seriously threatened the young church. They also denied the believer's only Master, the Lord Jesus Christ.

A teaching outline for the book of Jude is as follows along with suggestions for dealing with each section.

Introduction

Jude, the author, though a half-brother of Jesus, identified himself simply as a bondservant of Jesus. Jesus lived in a divided home in that some members of the family did not accept Him as their Savior until after His resurrection.

Observe all the triads Jude uses in this short letter.

Discuss the other matters mentioned in the introduction to the epistle and the first two verses.

Use an illustration of defending something or someone. From this, point out that Jude urged his readers to contend for the historic Christian faith.

I. Exhortation to Contend for the Faith (Jude 1:3-4)

Jude intended to write to those he loved in Christ about the common salvation they shared together. The Spirit of God had other plans, however; He wanted Jude to warn about false teaching instead.

Emphasize the need today to contend for the faith but not to be contentious while doing it. False teachers were circulating their false doctrines. False teachers still do the same today.

You may want to use some of the other scriptural warnings about false doctrine (see the commentary on verses 3 and 4).

II. Examples of Unbelief in the Past (Jude 1:5–7)

Like the original readers of this little epistle, people in the twenty-first century need to be reminded of how God dealt with false teachers in the past. Three illustrations are given in these verses of how God judged false teaching and wicked behavior. Briefly explain each of these.

III. Explanations of the Behavior of the False Teachers (Jude 1:8–19)

Highlight how God through Jude describes the false teachers and their teaching. Jude likens the behavior of the false teachers among his readers to the characters in his three examples of unbelief—Cain, Balaam, and Korah.

Be familiar with these examples so that you can explain briefly the specific sin in each case.

Observe how many different ways Jude describes the false teachers (vv. 12–16). Compare the behavior of the false teachers with the way Satan deceives. He too always appears to be other than he really is.

IV. Encouragement for Believers (Jude 1:20–25)

Jude turns his attention back to the "beloved" ones to whom he was writing—"But you" (v. 20).

God's Word was the sure source of victory for these people, and it still is for us today. Stress the need to be in the Word on a regular basis and to memorize it.

While the children of God stand firm in the Word of God, they should also seek to salvage others who are entrapped in false teaching. Jude exhorts his readers—and us—to be reaching out to those who do not know the truth.

Conclusion and Application

Give a short synopsis of Jude's teaching. Stress for the believers the need to do what Jude called upon his original readers to do in verses 20 and 21.

Do not miss the opportunity to give a clear presentation of the gospel as you conclude the message.

Bibliography

First John

Brown, Raymond E. *The Epistles of John.* The Anchor Bible. Garden City, NY: Doubleday, 1982.

Bruce, F. F. *The Epistles of St. John.* Old Tappan, NJ: Revell, 1970.

Hodges, Zane C. *The Epistles of John.* Irving, TX: Grace Evangelical Society, 1999.

Hodges, Zane C. *1 John.* The Bible Knowledge Commentary. Edited by John F. Walvoord and Roy B. Zuck. Wheaton, IL: Victor Books, 1983.

Johnson, Thomas F. *1, 2, and 3 John.* New International Bible Commentary. Edited by W. Ward Gasque. Peabody, MA: Hendrickson, 1993.

Lenski, R. C. H. *The Interpretation of the Epistles of St. Peter, St. John, and St. Jude.* Minneapolis: Augsburg, 1966.

Robertson, Archibald Thomas. *Word Pictures in the New Testament.* Vol. 6 Nashville: Broadman, 1933.

Ryrie, Charles Caldwell. *Epistles of John.* Wycliffe Bible Commentary. Chicago: Moody Press, 1992.

Showers, Renald E. *There Really Is a Difference.* Bellmawr, NJ: The Friends of Israel Gospel Ministry, 1990.

Smalley, Stephen S. *1, 2, 3 John.* World Biblical Commentary. Vol. 51. Waco, TX: Word, 1984.

Stott, John R. W. *The Epistles of John.* Grand Rapids: Eerdmans, 1974.

Westcott, Brooke Foss. *The Epistles of St. John.* Grand Rapids: Eerdmans, 1952.

Wuest, Kenneth S. *In These Last Days.* Grand Rapids: Eerdmans, 1954.

Second John

Carson, D. A., Douglas J. Moo, and Leon Morris. *An Introduction to the New Testament*. Grand Rapids: Zondervan, 1992.

Hodges, Zane C. *The Epistles of John*. Irving, TX: Grace Evangelical Society, 1999.

Smalley, Stephen S. *1, 2, 3 John*. World Biblical Commentary. Vol. 51. Waco, TX: Word, 1984.

Stott, John R. W. *The Epistles of John*. Grand Rapids: Eerdmans, 1974.

Westcott, Brooke Foss. *The Epistles of St. John*. Grand Rapids: Eerdmans Publishing Company, 1952.

Third John

Brown, Raymond E. *The Epistles of John*. The Anchor Bible. Garden City, NY: Doubleday, 1982.

Hodges, Zane C. *The Epistles of John*. Irving, TX: Grace Evangelical Society, 1999.

Smalley, Stephen S. *1, 2, 3 John*. World Biblical Commentary. Vol. 51. Waco, TX: Word, 1984.

Stott, John R. W. *The Epistles of John*. Grand Rapids: Eerdmans, 1974.

Jude

Green, Michael. *The Second Epistle of Peter and the Epistle of Jude*. Edited by R. V. G. Tasker. Grand Rapids: Eerdmans, 1973.

Lange, J. P. *Commentary on the Holy Scriptures—Jude*. Grand Rapids: Zondervan, 1960.

Lenski, R. C. H. *The Interpretation of the Epistles of St. Peter, St. John, and St. Jude*. Minneapolis: Augsburg, 1966.

Mayor, Joseph. *The Epistle of St. Jude*. Grand Rapids: Baker, 1965.

Robertson, Archibald Thomas. *Word Pictures in the New Testament*. Vol. 6 Nashville: Broadman, 1933.

Wuest, Kenneth S. *In These Last Days*. Grand Rapids: Eerdmans, 1954.

Notes

Chapter 1—Introduction to First John

1. Everett F. Harrison, *Introduction to the New Testament* (Grand Rapids: Eerdmans, 1974), 438–39.
2. Charles John Ellicott, *Commentary on the Whole Bible*, 8 vols. (Grand Rapids: Zondervan, 1959), 8:468.
3. Ibid.
4. Henry Clarence Thiessen, *Introduction to the New Testament* (Grand Rapids: Eerdmans, 1958), 307.
5. See Zane C. Hodges, *1 John*, The Bible Knowledge Commentary, ed. John F. Walvoord and Roy B. Zuck (Wheaton, IL: Victor Books, 1983), 882.
6. Harrison, *Introduction to the New Testament*, 447.
7. Roy B. Zuck, *A Biblical Theology of the New Testament* (Chicago: Moody Press, 1994), 227.
8. Ibid., 228.
9. Harrison, *Introduction to the New Testament*, 443.
10. Ibid., 440.
11. Ibid., 439.
12. Albert Barnes, *Notes on the New Testament*, 14 vols. (Grand Rapids: Baker, 1983), 13:277.

Chapter 2—Fellowship with God

1. Albert Barnes, *Notes on the New Testament*, 14 vols. (Grand Rapids: Baker, 1983), 13:278.

2. Ibid., 13:279.

3. Tom Wilson and Keith Stapley, eds., *What the Bible Teaches*. 6 vols. (Kilmarnock, Scotland: John Ritchie, 1987), 189.

4. Kenneth S. Wuest, *In These Last Days* (Grand Rapids: Eerdmans, 1954), 94.

5. Barnes, *Notes on the New Testament*, 13:281.

6. Zane C. Hodges, *The Epistles of John* (Irving, TX: Grace Evangelical Society, 1999), 51.

7. John R. W. Stott, *The Epistles of John* (Grand Rapids: Eerdmans, 1974), 71.

8. Some understand 1 John 1:6 to be describing an unsaved person. See, for example, Wuest, *In These Last Days*, 101–2. The context of the verse is better satisfied, however, by seeing the reference to believers. For a fuller discussion of this approach, see Hodges, *The Epistles of John*, 59–60.

9. Hodges, *The Epistles of John*, 61.

Chapter 3—Sin and the Child of God

1. Zane C. Hodges, *The Epistles of John* (Irving, TX: Grace Evangelical Society, 1999), 37.

2. For example, see Kenneth S. Wuest, *In These Last Days* (Grand Rapids: Eerdmans, 1954); Archibald Thomas Robertson, *Word Pictures in the New Testament*, vol. 6 (Nashville: Broadman, 1933); and John R. W. Stott, *The Epistles of John* (Grand Rapids: Eerdmans, 1974).

3. Wuest, *In These Last Days*, 106.

4. Hodges, *The Epistles of John*, 65.

5. Ibid., 71.

6. Albert Barnes, *Notes on the New Testament*, 14 vols. (Grand Rapids: Baker, 1983), 13:291.

7. Mal Couch, "Calvinism: Five or Four Points?" *The Conservative Theological Journal* (Ft. Worth, TX) 4, no. 12 (August 2000), 206.

8. For a full discussion of the contrasts between covenantism and dispensationalism, see Renald E. Showers, *There Really Is a Difference* (Bellmawr, NJ: The Friends of Israel Gospel Ministry, 1990).

9. Wuest, *In These Last Days*, 112.

Chapter 4—Fellowship with God and the Believer's Walk

1. R. C. H. Lenski, *The Interpretation of the Epistles of St. Peter, St. John, and St. Jude* (Minneapolis: Augsburg, 1966), 413.

2. Albert Barnes, *Notes on the New Testament*, 14 vols. (Grand Rapids: Baker, 1983), 13:294.

3. Zane C. Hodges, *The Epistles of John* (Irving, TX: Grace Evangelical Society, 1999), 94.

4. Kenneth S. Wuest, *In These Last Days* (Grand Rapids: Eerdmans, 1954), 124.

5. Barnes, *Notes on the New Testament*, 13:297.

6. See F. F. Bruce, *The Epistles of St. John* (Old Tappan, NJ: Revell, 1970), 60–64, for fuller treatment of its uses in John's writings.

7. Brooke Foss Westcott, *The Epistles of St. John* (Grand Rapids: Eerdmans, 1952), 63.

8. Hodges, *The Epistles of John*, 102.

Chapter 5—Antichrists in the Last Hour

1. Zane C. Hodges, *The Epistles of John* (Irving, TX: Grace Evangelical Society, 1999), 109.

2. Albert Barnes, *Notes on the New Testament*, 14 vols. (Grand Rapids: Baker, 1983), 13:301.

3. Archibald Thomas Robertson, *Word Pictures in the New Testament*, 6 vols. (Nashville: Broadman, 1933), 6:215.

4. Thomas F. Johnson, *1, 2, and 3 John*, New International Biblical Commentary. W. Ward Gasque, ed. (Peabody, MA: Hendrickson, 1993), 57.

5. Barnes, *Notes on the New Testament*, 13:305–6.

6. Ibid., 13:305.

7. Brooke Foss Westcott, *The Epistles of St. John* (Grand Rapids: Eerdmans, 1952), 77.

8. Raymond E. Brown, *The Epistles of John*, The Anchor Bible (Garden City, NY: Doubleday, 1982), 355.

Chapter 6—Fellowship with the Lord and His Return

1. Kenneth S. Wuest, *In These Last Days* (Grand Rapids: Eerdmans, 1954); 138 translates the phrase, "whenever He is made visible."

2. John R. W. Stott, *The Epistles of John* (Grand Rapids: Eerdmans, 1974), 116–17.

3. Glenn W. Barker, "1 John," in *The Expositor's Bible Commentary*, ed. Frank E. Gaebelein, 12 vols. (Grand Rapids: Zondervan, 1981), 12:330.

4. Ibid., 12:331.

5. Henry Alford, *The Greek Testament*, 4 vols. (Chicago: Moody Press, 1958), 4:463.

Chapter 7—Sins, the Savior, and the Sons of God

1. Zane C. Hodges, *The Epistles of John* (Irving, TX: Grace Evangelical Society, 1999), 132.

2. Albert Barnes, *Notes on the New Testament*, 14 vols. (Grand Rapids: Baker, 1983), 13:315.

3. Tom Wilson and Keith Stapley, eds., *What the Bible Teaches*, 9 vols. (Kilmarnock, Scotland: John Ritchie, 1987), 5:222.

4. John R. W. Stott, *The Epistles of John* (Grand Rapids: Eerdmans, 1974), 131–35. Stott responds to each of these views I here summarize. He presents his own preference by appealing to the present tenses: "does not practice sin" in 2:6 and "cannot continue sinning" in 2:9. See also Raymond E. Brown, *The Epistles of John*, The Anchor Bible (Garden City, NY: Doubleday, 1982), for listing and discussion.

5. Hodges, *The Epistles of John*, 134–44, seems to do this with the present tense. Yet he does concede that "there is no doubt that in an appropriate context the Greek present tense can have a present progressive force like "he is sinning" (p. 143). He simply does not believe the present tense issue is appropriate in this context. I believe it is.

6. Ibid., 134.

7. Ibid., 136.

8. Charles Caldwell Ryrie, *Ryrie Study Bible*, expanded ed. (Chicago: Moody Press, 1995), 1995.

9. Wilson and Stapley, *What the Bible Teaches*, 5:223.

10. Archibald Thomas Robertson, *Word Pictures in the New Testament*, 6 vols. (Nashville: Broadman, 1933), 6:223.

11. Ibid.

12. Stephen S. Smalley, *1, 2, 3 John* (vol. 51), Word Biblical Commentary (Waco, TX: Word, 1984), 223.

13. Kenneth S. Wuest, *In These Last Days* (Grand Rapids: Eerdmans, 1954), 150.

14. Wilson and Stapley, *What the Bible Teaches*, 5:225.

Chapter 8—Hate and Love

1. Brooke Foss Westcott, *The Epistles of St. John* (Grand Rapids: Eerdmans, 1952), 112.

2. This is by far the majority opinion and interpretation of this passage. Hodges, *The Epistles of John* (Irving, TX: Grace Evangelical Society, 1999), has a different understanding. He takes the view that the Christian who does not love the brethren is "*abiding in death* in the sense that he has lost touch with the experience of God's life" (cf. pp. 158–59).

3. Tom Wilson and Keith Stapley, eds., *What the Bible Teaches*, 9 vols. (Kilmarnock, Scotland: John Ritchie, 1987), 5:231.

4. Zane C. Hodges, *The Epistles of John* (Irving, TX: Grace Evangelical Society, 1999), 168.

Chapter 9—Exhortations to the Beloved

1. See Zane C. Hodges, *The Epistles of John* (Irving, TX: Grace Evangelical Society, 1999), Raymond E. Brown, *The Epistles of John*, The Anchor Bible (Garden City, NY: Doubleday, 1982).

2. Hodges, in *The Epistles of John*, uses this term to describe those John opposes.

3. Tom Wilson and Keith Stapley, eds., *What the Bible Teaches*, 9 vols. (Kilmarnock, Scotland: John Ritchie, 1987), 5:235.

4. Ibid., 5:237.

5. Kenneth S. Wuest, *In These Last Days* (Grand Rapids: Eerdmans, 1954), 163.

6. Ibid.

7. Archibald Thomas Robertson, *Word Pictures in the New Testament*, 6 vols. (Nashville: Broadman, 1933), 6:232.

8. Wilson and Stapley, *What the Bible Teaches*, 5:239.

Chapter 10—Union with God and Unity among the Brethren

1. Brooke Foss Westcott, *The Epistles of St. John* (Grand Rapids: Eerdmans, 1952), 151.

2. Zane C. Hodges, *The Epistles of John* (Irving, TX: Grace Evangelical Society, 1999), 193.

3. Tom Wilson and Keith Stapley, eds., *What the Bible Teaches*, 9 vols. (Kilmarnock, Scotland: John Ritchie, 1987), 5:247.

4. Archibald Thomas Robertson, *Word Pictures in the New Testament*, vols. (Nashville: Broadman, 1933), 6:234.

5. Wilson and Stapley, *What the Bible Teaches*, 5:243.

6. R. C. H. Lenski, *The Interpretation of the Epistles of St. Peter, St. John, and St. Jude* (Minneapolis: Augsburg, 1966), 513.

Chapter 11–Believers as Overcomers

1. Brooke Foss Westcott, *The Epistles of St. John* (Grand Rapids: Eerdmans, 1952), 176.

2. Zane C. Hodges, *The Epistles of John* (Irving, TX: Grace Evangelical Society, 1999), 216.

Chapter 12–The Father's Testimony of the Son

1. Stephen S. Smalley, *1, 2, 3 John* (vol. 51), Word Biblical Commentary (Waco, TX: Word, 1984), 289.

Chapter 13–A Call to Action

1. Stephen S. Smalley, *1, 2, 3 John* (Vol. 51), Word Biblical Commentary (Waco, TX: Word, 1984), 303.

2. John R. W. Stott, *The Epistles of John* (Grand Rapids: Eerdmans, 1974), 191–92.

3. Zane C. Hodges, *The Epistles of John* (Irving, TX: Grace Evangelical Society, 1999), 242.

4. Ibid.

5. Glenn W. Barker, "1, 2, 3 John," in *The Expositor's Bible Commentary*, ed. Frank E. Gaebelein, 12 vols. (Grand Rapids: Zondervan, 1981), 12:357.

6. John Gill, *An Exposition of the New Testament*, 6 vols. (Grand Rapids: Baker, 1980), 6:912.

Chapter 14–A Challenge to the Children of God

1. R. C. H. Lenski, *The Interpretation of the Epistles of St. Peter, St. John, and St. Jude* (Minneapolis: Augsburg, 1966), 545.

2. Robert Tuck, *The Preacher's Complete Homiletic Commentary,* 31 vols. (Grand Rapids: Baker, n.d.), 31:345.

3. Henry Alford, *The Greek Testament,* 4 vols. (Chicago: Moody Press, 1958), 4:515.

4. Frank E. Gaebelein, gen. ed., *The Expositor's Bible Commentary,* 12 Vols. (Grand Rapids: Zondervan, 1981), 12:357

Chapter 15—Introduction to Second John

1. Zane C. Hodges, The Epistles of John (Irving, TX: Grace Evangelical Society, 1999), 21. For further documentation of Johannine authorship, see D. A. Carson, Douglas J. Moo, and Leon Morris, An Introduction to the New Testament (Grand Rapids: Zondervan, 1992), 139–43, 446–50.

2. Hodges, *The Epistles of John,* 27, argues, however, that the three epistles were written from Jerusalem.

3. Ibid.

4. Everett F. Harrison, *Introduction to the New Testament* (Grand Rapids: Eerdmans, 1974), 452–53.

5. See discussion of both views in John R. W. Stott, *The Epistles of John* (Grand Rapids: Eerdmans, 1974), 200–201.

6. R. C. H. Lenski, *The Interpretation of the Three Epistles of John* (Minneapolis, MN: Augsburg, 1966), 552.

Chapter 16—Responsive Love

1. R. C. H. Lenski, *The Interpretation of the Epistles of St. Peter, St. John, and St. Jude* (Minneapolis: Augsburg, 1966), 554.

2. Ibid., 200.

3. Albert Barnes, *Notes on the New Testament,* 14 vols. (Grand Rapids: Baker, 1983), 13:361.

4. Simon J. Kistemaker, *James and I–III John* (Grand Rapids: Baker, 1992), 375.

5. Ibid., 375–76.

Chapter 17—Obedient Love

1. Stephen S. Smalley, *1, 2, 3 John* (vol. 51), Word Biblical Commentary (Waco, TX: Word, 1984), 324.

2. John R. W. Stott, *The Epistles of John* (Grand Rapids: Eerdmans, 1974), 201.

3. Zane C. Hodges, *The Epistles of John* (Irving, TX: Grace Evangelical Society, 1999), 258.

4. R. C. H. Lenski, *The Interpretation of the Epistles of St. Peter, St. John, and St. Jude* (Minneapolis: Augsburg, 1966), 564.

Chapter 18—Discerning Love

1. R. C. H. Lenski, *The Interpretation of the Epistles of St. Peter, St. John, and St. Jude* (Minneapolis: Augsburg, 1966), 566.

2. Simon J. Kistemaker, *James and I–III John* (Grand Rapids: Baker, 1992), 380.

3. Brook Foss Westcott, *The Epistles of St. John* (Grand Rapids: Eerdmans, 1952), 230.

4. Ibid., 264.

5. Henry Alford, *The Greek Testament*, 4 vols. (Chicago: Moody Press, 1958), 4:521.

6. Lenski, *The Interpretation of the Epistles of St. Peter, St. John, and St. Jude*, 572–73.

7. Kistemaker, *James and I–III John*, 386.

Chapter 19—Introduction to Third John

1. See Zane C. Hodges, *The Epistles of John* (Irving, TX: Grace Evangelical Society, 1999), 23–28.

2. Everett F. Harrison, *Introduction to the New Testament* (Grand Rapids: Eerdmans, 1974), 450.

Chapter 20—The Response of Gaius to Truth

1. Simon J. Kistemaker, *James and I–III John* (Grand Rapids: Baker, 1992), 389.

2. R. C. H. Lenski, *The Interpretation of the Epistles of St. Peter, St. John, and St. Jude* (Minneapolis: Augsburg, 1966), 577.

3. See Kenneth S. Wuest, *In These Last Days* (Grand Rapids, Eerdmans, 1954), 217, where he documents this from Adolph Deissmann, *Light from the Ancient East*, trans. by L. R. M. Strahan (New York: Doran), 1927.

4. Albert Barnes, *Notes on the New Testament,* 14 vols. (Grand Rapids: Baker, 1983), 13:372.

5. Zane C. Hodges, *The Epistles of John* (Irving, TX: Grace Evangelical Society, 1999), 281–82.

6. Kistemaker, *James and I–III John,* 393.

7. Stephen S. Smalley, *1, 2, 3 John* (vol. 51), Word Biblical Commentary (Waco, TX: Word Books), 1984, 351.

Chapter 21—The Response of Diotrephes to Truth

1. Simon J. Kistemaker, *James and I–III John* (Grand Rapids: Baker, 1992), 396.

2. Raymond E. Brown, *The Epistles of John,* The Anchor Bible (Garden City, NY: Doubleday, 1982), 746–47.

3. R. C. H. Lenski, *The Interpretation of the Epistles of St. Peter, St. John, and St. Jude* (Minneapolis: Augsburg, 1966), 588.

4. Kenneth S. Wuest, *In These Last Days* (Grand Rapids: Eerdmans, 1954), 223, citing grammarians A. T. Robertson and Dana and Mantey in support of this.

5. John R. W. Stott, *The Epistles of John* (Grand Rapids: Eerdmans, 1974), 228.

6. Kistemaker, *James and I–III John,* 399.

Chapter 22—The Response of Demetrius to Truth

1. Henry Alford, *The Greek Testament,* 4 vols. (Chicago: Moody Press, 1958), 4:527.

2. Simon J. Kistemaker, *James and I–III John* (Grand Rapids: Baker, 1992), 402.

Chapter 23—Introduction to Jude

1. Henry Clarence Thiessen, *Introduction to the New Testament* (Grand Rapids: Eerdmans, 1958), 293–94.

2. R. C. H. Lenski, *The Interpretation of the Epistles of St. Peter, St. John, and St. Jude* (Minneapolis: Augsburg, 1966), 597.

3. Simon J. Kistemaker, *Peter and Jude* (Grand Rapids: Baker, 1993), 357.

4. A. T. Robertson, *Word Pictures in the New Testament*, 6 Vols., (Nashville, TN: Broadman, 1933), 6:183-84.

5. R. C. H. Lenski, *The Interpretation of the Epistles of St. Peter, St. John, and St. Jude*, 599.

6. Thiessen, *Introduction to the New Testament*, 295.

7. Edwin A. Blum, "Jude," in *The Expositor's Bible Commentary*, ed. Frank E. Gaebelein 12 vols. (Grand Rapids: Zondervan, 1981), 12:385.

8. Martin Luther, *Commentary on Peter & Jude*, Translated by John Nichols Lenker (Grand Rapids: Kregel, 1982), 290.

9. Simon J. Kistemaker, *Peter and Jude*, p. 361.

10. John Calvin, *Commentaries on the Catholic Epistles: The Epistle of Jude*, Editor and translator, John Owen (Grand Rapids: Eerdmans, 1948), 427.

11. E. Hennecke, W. Schneemelcher, and R. Wilson, eds., *New Testament Apocrypha*, 2 Vols. (London: Lutterworth, 1963), 1:44–45.

12. Mal Couch, gen. ed., *The Conservative Theological Journal*, Vol. 4, No. 13. Mal Couch, "Inerrancy: The General Epistles" (Ft. Worth, TX: Tyndale Theological Seminary, Dec. 2000), 343.

13. R. C. H. Lenski, *The Interpretation of the Epistles of St. Peter, St. John, and St. Jude*, 603.

Chapter 24–Salutation and Warning about False Teachers

1. Mal Couch, gen. ed., *A Bible Handbook to the Book of the Apostles* (Grand Rapids: Kregel, 1999), 193-94.

2. Henry C. Thiessen, *Introduction to the New Testament* (Grand Rapids: Eerdmans, 1958), 294.

3. R. C. H. Lenski, *The Interpretation of the Epistles of St. Peter, St. John, and St. Jude* (Minneapolis: Augsburg, 1966), 608.

4. Ibid., 609.

5. Simon J. Kistemaker, *Peter and Jude* (Grand Rapids: Baker, 1993), 374.

6. Thomas Manton, *Commentary on Jude* (Grand Rapids: Kregel, 1988), 133.

7. Marvin R. Vincent, *Word Studies in the New Testament*, 4 Vols. (New York: Charles Scribner's, 1906) 1:689.

Chapter 25–Explanations about False Teachers

1. Kenneth S. Wuest, *In These Last Days* (Grand Rapids: Eerdmans, 1954), 239.

2. Albert Barnes, *Notes on the New Testament*, 14 Vols. (Grand Rapids: Baker, 1983), 13:391.

3. John F. Walvoord and Roy B. Zuck, eds., *The Bible Knowledge Commentary* (Wheaton: Victor Books, 1983), 920.

4. Robert Lightner, *Angels, Satan, and Demons* (Nashville: Word, 1998), 101.

5. Harold G. Stigers, *A Commentary on Genesis* (Grand Rapids: Zondervan, 1976), 98.

6. H. C. Leupold, *Exposition of Genesis* (Columbus, OH: Wartburg, 1942), 251.

7. Henry M. Morris, *The Genesis Record* (Grand Rapids: Baker, 1994), 165.

8. R. C. H. Lenski, *The Interpretation of the Epistles of St. Peter, St. John, and St. Jude,* (Minneapolis: Augsburg, 1966), 622.

9. Archibald Thomas Robertson, *Word Pictures in the New Testament* (Nashville: Broadman, 1933), 6:189.

10. Merrill F. Unger, *Unger's Commentary on the Old Testament* (Chattanooga, TN: AMG Publishers, 2002), 66.

11. J. P. Lange, *Commentary on the Holy Scriptures—Jude* (Grand Rapids: Zondervan, 1960), 19.

12. Merrill F. Unger, *Introductory Guide to the Old Testament* (Grand Rapids: Zondervan, 1981), 85.]

13. R. C. H. Lenski, *The Interpretation of the Epistles of St. Peter, St. John, and St. Jude,* 629.

14. T. Wilson and K. Stapley, gen. eds. *What the Bible Teaches*, 9 Vols. (Kilmarnock, Scotland: John Ritchie, 1987), 5:311.

15. R. C. H. Lenski, *The Interpretation of the Epistles of St. Peter, St. John, and St. Jude* 632–33.

16. Michael Green, *2 Peter and Jude*, C. L. Morris, ed., Tyndale New Testament Commentaries, 19 Vols. (Grand Rapids: Eerdmans, 1973), 18:172.

17. Kenneth Barker, gen. ed., *The Wycliffe Exegetical Commentary*, R. K. Harrison, "Numbers" (Chicago: Moody, 1990), 234

18. Michael Green, *2 Peter and Jude*, 18:175.

19. Albert Barnes, *Notes on the New Testament*, 14 vols. (Grand Rapids: Baker, 1983), 13:401.

20. Simon J. Kistemaker, *Peter and Jude* (Grand Rapids: Baker, 1993), 15–16.

21. Michael Green, *2 Peter and Jude*, 18:194.

22. Martin Luther, *Commentary on Peter & Jude*, Translated by John Nichols Lenker (Grand Rapids: Kregel, 1982), 300.

Chapter 26—Exhortations and Encouragement for Believers

1. Albert Barnes, *Notes on the New Testament*, 14 vols. (Grand Rapids: Baker, 1983), 13:402.

2. Michael Green, *2 Peter and Jude*, C. L. Morris, ed., Tyndale New Testament Commentaries, 19 Vols. (Grand Rapids: Eerdmans, 1973), 18:181.

3. Simon J. Kistemaker, *Peter and Jude* (Grand Rapids: Baker, 1993), 404.

4. Thomas Manton, *Commentary on Jude* (Grand Rapids: Kregel, 1988), 335.

5. J. P. Lange, *Commentary on the Holy Scriptures—Jude* (Grand Rapids: Zondervan, 1960), 30.

6. Charles John Ellicott, ed., *Ellicott's Commentary on the Whole Bible*, 8 Vols. (Grand Rapids: Zondervan, 1959), 8:515.

7. R. C. H. Lenski, *The Interpretation of the Epistles of St. Peter, St. John, and St. Jude* (Minneapolis: Augsburg, 1966), 646.

8. Horst Balz and Gerhard Schneider, eds. *Exegetical Dictionary of the New Testament*, 3 Vols. (Grand Rapids: Zondervan, 1994), 1:306.

9. R. C. H. Lenski, *The Interpretation of the Epistles of St. Peter, St. John, and St. Jude*, 648–49.

10. Albert Barnes, *Notes on the New Testament*, 13:403.

11. Edwin A. Blum, "Jude," in *The Expositor's Bible Commentary*, ed. Frank E. Gaebelein, 12 vols. (Grand Rapids: Zondervan, 1981), 12:384.

12. Tom Wilson and Keith Stapley, eds., *What the Bible Teaches*, 9 vols. (Kilmarnock, Scotland: John Ritchie, 1987), 5:330.

13. H. G. Liddell and R. Scott, eds., *Greek-English Lexicon*, (Oxford: Clarendon Press, 1996), 231.

14. Michael Green, *2 Peter and Jude*, 18:206.

15. Simon J. Kistemaker, *Peter and Jude*, 413.

16. Horst Balz and Gerhard Schneider, *Exegetical Dictionary of the New Testament*, 2:10.

17. Thomas Manton, *Commentary on Jude* (Grand Rapids: Kregel, 1988), 381.

18. Lenski, *The Interpretation of the Epistles of St. Peter, St. John, and St. Jude*, 651.

Appendix 1—The Antichrist

1. Harry Bultema, *Commentary on Daniel* (Grand Rapids: Kregel, 1988), 287–89.

2. Mal Couch, *The Hope of Christ's Return* (Chattanooga, TN: AMG Publishers, 2001), 209.

3. Ibid., 211.

4. Ibid., 216.

5. Mal Couch, ed., *A Bible Handbook to Revelation* (Grand Rapids: Kregel, 2001), 234.

6. Raphael Patai, *The Messiah Texts* (Detroit: Wayne State University Press, 1979).

7. Midrash *waYoshea', BhM 1:56*.

8. Arnold G. Fruchtenbaum, *The Footsteps of the Messiah* (Tustin, CA: Ariel Press, 1990), 139–40.

9. Ibid., 141.

10. Ibid.

Appendix 2—The Doctrine of Confession

1. R. C. H. Lenski, *The Interpretation of the Epistles of St. Peter, St. John, and St. Jude* (Minneapolis: Augsburg, 1966), 566.

Appendix 3—John's Epistles and the Cult of Gnosticism

1. Trent C. Butler, ed., *Holman Bible Dictionary* (Nashville: Holman Bible Publishers, 1991), 559.

Appendix 5—Teaching Through First John

1. Note: The above information and the outline to follow come largely from an adult quarter of study written by this author published by Regular Baptist Press in Chicago in 1972.

About the Author

Robert P. Lightner is Professor Emeritus of Systematic Theology at Dallas Theological Seminary where he began serving the Lord in 1968. Dr. Lightner is also adjunct professor of theology at Tyndale Theological Seminary in Fort Worth, Texas. He holds a Th.B. from Baptist Bible Seminary, a Th.M. and Th.D. from Dallas Theological Seminary, and an M.L.A. from Southern Methodist University in Dallas. He is the author of numerous books on theology, apologetics, and prophecy, including *Sin, Salvation, and the Savior; The Handbook of Evangelical Theology;* and *The Death Christ Died.* He lives in Garland, Texas.

About the General Editors

Edward Hindson is Professor of Religion, Dean of the Institute of Biblical Studies, and Assistant to the Chancellor at Liberty University in Lynchburg, Virginia. He has authored several books and also has served as co-editor of the *Knowing Jesus Study Bible,* associate editor of the *Tim LaHaye Prophecy Study Bible,* contributor to *The Complete Bible Commentary,* and as one of the translators for the New King James Version. Dr. Hindson is a member of the executive committee of the "Pre-Trib Research Center" and has served as a guest lecturer at both Harvard and Oxford Universities.

Mal Couch is founder and president of Tyndale Theological Seminary and Biblical Institute in Fort Worth, Texas. He previously taught at Philadelphia College of the Bible, Moody Bible Institute, and Dallas Theological Seminary. His other publications include *The Hope of Christ's Return: A Premillennial Commentary on 1 and 2 Thessalonians, A Bible Handbook to Revelation,* and *Dictionary of Premillennial Theology.*